Alexander Viets Griswold Allen, Francis Greenwood Peabody

**The Message of Christ to Manhood**

being the William Belden Noble lectures for 1898

Alexander Viets Griswold Allen, Francis Greenwood Peabody

**The Message of Christ to Manhood**
*being the William Belden Noble lectures for 1898*

ISBN/EAN: 9783337369606

Printed in Europe, USA, Canada, Australia, Japan

Cover: Foto ©Lupo / pixelio.de

More available books at **www.hansebooks.com**

# THE MESSAGE OF CHRIST
# TO MANHOOD

BEING THE

### William Belden Noble Lectures

FOR 1898

BY

Rev. ALEXANDER V. G. ALLEN, D. D.
Rev. FRANCIS G. PEABODY, D. D.
Rev. THEODORE T. MUNGER, D. D.
Rev. WILLIAM DeW. HYDE, D. D.
Rev. HENRY VAN DYKE, D. D.
Rt. Rev. HENRY C. POTTER, D. D.

BOSTON AND NEW YORK
HOUGHTON, MIFFLIN AND COMPANY
The Riverside Press, Cambridge
1899

COPYRIGHT, 1898, BY HARVARD UNIVERSITY
ALL RIGHTS RESERVED

TO

THE STUDENTS

OF

HARVARD UNIVERSITY

Omne datum optimum, et omne donum perfectum desursum est, descendens a Patre luminum.

———◆———

The building of the perfect man is the noblest work that can go on in the world. It is the very crown of God's creation.

PHILLIPS BROOKS.

# NOTE

THE Lectures, of which this volume is the first, were constituted a perpetual foundation in Harvard University in 1898, as a memorial by his wife to the late William Belden Noble, of Washington, D. C., a member of the Class of 1885. In the appendix and elsewhere in this volume will be found a brief recital of the circumstances of his life and an appreciation of his character. By his untimely death in 1896 the work which he had at heart to perform in this world was to human vision left unfinished. These Lectures are intended to carry on that work in accordance with the comprehensive spiritual ideal he had set before him. Their purpose will be seen in the following citation from the deed of gift by which they were established:

"The object of the founder of the Lectures is to continue the mission of her husband. It was his supreme desire to extend the influence of Jesus as the way, the truth, and the life; to make known the meaning of the words of Jesus, — I am come that they might have life, and that they might have it more abundantly. In accordance with the large interpretation of the Influence of Jesus by the late Phillips Brooks, with whose religious teaching he in whose memory the Lectures are established and also the founder of the Lectures were in deep sympathy, it is intended that the scope of the Lectures shall be as wide as the highest interests of humanity. With this end in view, — the perfection of the spiritual man and the consecration by the spirit of Jesus of every department of human character, thought, and activity, the Lectures may include philosophy, literature, art, poetry, the natural sciences, political economy, sociology, ethics, history both civil and ecclesiastical, as well as theology and the more direct interests of the religious life. Beyond a sympathy with the purpose of the Lectures, as thus defined, no restriction is placed upon the lecturer."

CAMBRIDGE, November 5, 1898.

# CONTENTS

## I

THE MESSAGE OF CHRIST TO THE INDIVIDUAL MAN . 1
   By the Rev. ALEXANDER V. G. ALLEN, D.D., Professor of Ecclesiastical History in the Episcopal Theological School in Cambridge, Mass.

## II

THE MESSAGE OF CHRIST TO HUMAN SOCIETY . . 47
   By the Rev. FRANCIS G. PEABODY, D.D., Plummer Professor of Christian Morals in Harvard University.

## III

THE MESSAGE OF CHRIST TO THE WILL . . . . . 87
   By the Rev. THEODORE T. MUNGER, D.D., Minister of the United Church, New Haven, Conn.

## IV

THE MESSAGE OF CHRIST TO THE SCHOLAR . . . 115
   By the Rev. WILLIAM DEW. HYDE, D. D., President of Bowdoin College.

## V

THE MESSAGE OF CHRIST TO THE INNER LIFE . . 147
   By the Rev. HENRY VAN DYKE, D.D., Pastor of the Brick Church, New York, N. Y.

## VI

THE MESSAGE OF CHRIST TO THE FAMILY . . . . 183
   By the Rt. Rev. HENRY C. POTTER, D.D., Bishop of New York.

APPENDIX . . . . . . . . . . . . . . 205

# I

## THE MESSAGE OF CHRIST
## TO THE INDIVIDUAL MAN

By the Rev. ALEXANDER V. G. ALLEN, D.D.

# THE MESSAGE OF CHRIST TO THE INDIVIDUAL MAN

"I am come that they might have life and that they might have it more abundantly." — St. John x. 10.

A PECULIAR interest and solemnity belong to a moment like the present, when we are opening a new course of lectures in Harvard University, to be perpetuated in the coming generations. A woman out of devotion to the memory of her husband lays this new foundation. In order that it may be a service to the University and not a hindrance, she has been anxious that it should be free from accidental or transitory features of the age when it is established. But she has also requested that these lectures be associated with the name of Phillips Brooks, and if possible be given in the Phillips Brooks House now in process of erection on the grounds of the University as its memorial to the great preacher. She has made these conditions of her gift in the conviction that one who moved so powerfully his own age by his life and teaching must appeal to every age and always remain an impressive witness to the Gospel of Christ.

The objection may here be raised that it is not wise to associate that which we hope will be enduring, with the name of any individual, however great his reputation or his influence in his own day and generation. Is not the unwritten constitution, it may be said, more flexible, more capable of adaptation to the changing circumstances of thought and life than any document which sharply defines in letters the end to be attained. The written constitution is in danger of becoming a dead letter, or it must be revised in order to meet the expansion of human development. Even Magna Charta is now a document somewhat difficult to understand, when we attempt to trace in its antiquated provisions the spirit from whence has come the larger fruits of English freedom. Or in the ages nearer to our own, how many endowed lectureships now seem remote and inappropriate, so that only by some larger interpretation of their purpose than the founder held can they be made available to existing needs. Those who are charged with the administration of trust funds are rightly jealous of restrictions, which, however natural and intelligible when they were exacted, may become impossible at a later day.

There is undoubtedly a danger here and a difficulty to be met. But, over against it, is to be placed the common humanity which never greatly changes; so that it has been said of the Founder of our religion, — Jesus Christ, the same yesterday, to-day, and forever. And again, it is the distinctive merit of religious foundations and of university lectureships that they serve the purpose of holding the generations together, in order that the present age shall not be allowed to forget the service rendered to it by the past. They recall the difficulties which beset our forefathers, their problems with their imperfect solutions, their achievements also, and their victories. It is by no means a misfortune, that we should be forced to contemplate such monuments of the last century as the Dudleian Lectures at Harvard, or in England the Boyle Lectures, the Hulsean, or the Bampton. If the issues they represent seem remote, it may also be that they have not received their full solution. Such monuments are pathetic appeals from an earlier to a later generation, to remember its struggles for truth, or to come to its rescue by fulfilling its imperfect effort, or to explain and to justify its purpose.

Thus, for example, in the eighteenth century it was clearly perceived that there was a difference between natural theology, or that knowledge of God and of the moral law which the intelligence of man might read in the vision and order of external nature; and, on the other hand, what is called revealed theology, or that thought and knowledge of God which has its source in the deeper phases of human experience, wherein God is speaking within the soul. Here was the problem which the eighteenth century bequeathed to its successor, — How is the Deity speaking within the soul to be harmonized with the Deity disclosed in the life of external nature.

We too in this nineteenth century have been laboring with a religious problem, distinctly our own. The century will end before its solution is fully manifest. Already have other questions arisen, absorbing the attention of the hour, threatening to banish into forgetfulness some of the deeper issues of human life, for which the nineteenth century has stood. Phillips Brooks bore his part in the life of his age, and as a child of his age spoke to it with authority and power. It is with his teaching for his own time that I am to be occupied in part this evening, — " The Message of Christ to the Individual Man." But before turning to speak of Phillips Brooks, as a signal instance of the power of Christ inspiring the individual soul, let me cite one section from the charter of this new lectureship, and in so doing bring my subject more clearly before you.

" *The object of the founder is to continue the work of William Belden Noble, whose supreme desire was to extend the influence of Jesus as 'the Way, and the Truth, and the Life,' and to make known the meaning of His words, 'I am come that they might have Life, and that they might have it more abundantly.' In accordance with the large interpretation of these words by the late Phillips Brooks, with whose religious teaching he in whose memory the Lectures are established and the founder were in deep sympathy, it is intended that the scope of the Lectures shall be as wide as the highest interests of humanity. With this end in view, — the perfection of the spiritual man and the consecration by the spirit of Jesus of every department of human thought and learning, — the Lectures may include philosophy, literature, art, poetry, science, political economy, sociology, ethics, history both civil and ecclesiastical, as well as theology and the more direct interests of the religious life. Beyond a sympathy with the purpose of the Lectures as thus defined no restriction is placed upon the Lecturer."*

There were some things for which Phillips Brooks contended with so great earnestness that they constituted his distinctive mission to his age. Among these stood foremost the value of personality. The word has now come into more general use than when he began to illustrate and enforce its meaning. In his sermons he dwelt upon the personality of Christ as the ground of His claim to the obedience of men. There was one passage among the sayings of Christ which seemed to him the summary of the gospel: I am the Way, the Truth, and the Life. As he studied their meaning he came to see that in these words there was a gradation and a climax. If Christ was the way, it was because He was the truth. If He was the truth, it was because He was first the life. To the life or the personality of Christ belonged the pre-eminence. In that lay His power over the world.

When Phillips Brooks began his ministry he encountered here a difficulty. It was common enough to point men to Christ as the "way," as having given ethical precepts which would serve for the guidance of men. The Sermon on the Mount had never been wholly forgotten, in any age of the church, but in the first half of the nineteenth century it had been brought forth from its obscurity and enforced as the essence of the way of salvation. There were others who dwelt upon Christ as a teacher of the truth, as one who was Himself occupied with the highest problems of life. But as men turned over His ethical teaching, or the truth He offered about the relations of God and man, the question arose as to whether His doctrine were original with Him, or had not been anticipated in large extent by other teachers. The inference seemed inevitable that if the utterances of Christ were not new, His authority as an inspired teacher was impaired. In the middle of the nineteenth century there was great weakness upon this point. Thus it was said that ethical precept and spiritual truth carried their own evidence to the conscience and intellect, whether they came from Christ or from other men. The person of the teacher was of no especial importance. What Christ taught as true would be just as true if it came from Herod or from Catiline.

But the difficulty went further and deeper. There were students of the life and time of Christ who found it an open question whether He had ever existed. If there had been no such person at all, it was then argued, the course of history would not have been affected. Currents of thought and feeling, ideal creations of the human spirit, these had met at a great juncture in history and given birth to the Christian church. This peculiar difficulty which confronted men in the middle of the nineteenth century originated long before. When the historian Gibbon undertook to explain the growth of Christianity in the early centuries he had found sufficient cause in the zeal of the early Christians, in their profound belief in immortality, in their practice of the highest virtues, in their spirit of brotherly love. But Gibbon stopped there; he did not ask how or whence this belief or zeal had come.

It was distinctive of Phillips Brooks that on this point, which was a source of confusion and weakness, he held that truth and precept could have no weight, no authority, unless it were first embodied in a life. Only through a life could truth be manifested and propagated with power. If truth was to become converted into motive power, it must be through the alembic of personality. As he looked out on the world of men with whom he came in contact, or as he looked into himself, he saw that the one thing most needed was to make the truth, which men were holding or believing, available as power for the transmutation of character. There was adequate knowledge of the principles of right living, there was no doubt as to what the will of God required, but there was some obstacle which hindered belief and conviction from passing over into motive that would transform the soul.

In one of his earlier sermons he was working out this problem for himself.

"It seems to me," he there says, "that the source of all the trouble we have been speaking of lies in this, — the absence of a personal aspect from the truths we hold. I maintain that always, and never more than just to-day, owing no doubt to some special mental characteristics of our time, there is a tendency among men to seek after pure and abstract truth, truth entirely divested of personal relations. And I maintain that all such impersonal truth when it is acquired, however much it may do for sharpening and stocking the brains and improving the outward conditions of mankind, is as bad as useless, so far as any immediate effect upon the character and temperament is concerned. . . . How very rare a thing it is for pure and abstract truth to influence action, or to create or calm strong passions! It is truth, brought through a personal medium, cast into personal shapes, filled with true personal color, that either changes the simple character, or breaks off at a sharp angle the great world's course, or sends it hurrying in some new direction. . . . It is all very well to say 'Principles, not men.' It is principles brought to bear through the medium of manhood that rule the world. . . . To send out principles without men is to send a thin army of ghosts abroad who would make all virtue and manliness as shadowy and impalpable as themselves. . . . The personality of Jesus Christ is the medium through which abstract truth passes, and is turned into strength and resolution and action and comfort. Because He is also the *way* and *the life*."

It was another characteristic principle of Phillips Brooks that life could only proceed from life. This was the supreme presupposition which underlay the development of his own character as a man, controlling his thought and judgment concerning men, the clue also to the interpretation of human history. Among the sayings of Jesus regarding Himself, there was one passage which was constantly recurring in his sermons, — "I am come that they might have life, and that they might have it more abundantly." In the first sermon which he wrote upon this text, he was struck with the fact how constantly the word "life" was on the lips of Jesus. It was a word introducing us into the very heart of the teaching of Jesus : —

"He would have men saved from these alternatives, from degenerating into machines or into brutes. Life was what He was always praising, always promising. 'If thou wilt enter into life, keep my commandments.' 'He that believeth on me hath life.' 'As the Father hath life in Himself, so hath He given to the Son to have life in Himself.' 'Because I *live*, ye shall *live* also.' 'Ye will not come unto me that ye might have life.'

"The definition of 'life' as given by Jesus is that it

consists in goodness. Goodness is life, wickedness is death. 'The soul that sinneth, it shall die,' is not a threat, but rather the statement of a truth. For the soul that sinneth dies in its sinning, because for a human soul there is no life but in righteousness. Just so far as a man ceases to be good, he ceases to be a man.

"It is a popular phrase, 'To err is human.' There may be some truth in it, but it is a superficial truth. Christ says that to do right is human, and declares the profounder truth that the purpose and nature of humanity is to do right.

"The young man goes into reckless dissipation, and calls it seeing life to see or indulge in vice. But Christ calls it death. He that liveth in pleasure is dead while he liveth. To sin is to weaken the vitality."

But now comes the question of primary importance, How is this life, which consists in goodness, to be attained? Phillips Brooks made many contributions of his own to the interpretation of the meaning of life. But among them all, the answer he gave to this question takes the precedence. It was not with him merely a speculative question, nor did he study it for the purpose of an effective rhetoric in the pulpit. It was first and foremost the problem of his own soul. His answer to it becomes the key to his own experience, and enables us to know the man himself. Let me give the answer in his own words from an unpublished sermon on this same text, "I am come that they might have life."

"It is strange," he says, "to think how man's mind has always held by the idea that life was transmitted but not created. It has held it to be true of life in all its grades, even in the most palpable physical life. Man has an instinctive dislike to a notion of spontaneous generation. It seems to break into fragments his notion of vitality. The child's life is a perpetuation of the father's. Each generation transmutes the vitality of the generation before it into some new shape. Men used to dream that they might take the red blood out of a strong man's arm to reinforce a sick man's failing strength. And so of higher forms of vitality. Skill passes from teacher to scholar. Each new workman does not discover for himself his methods; he finds them already the property of this humanity into which he has been born. Courage passes from the strong heart to the weak heart as they press each other in a human embrace. Enthusiasm springs from eye to eye, as the spark leaps from one electric point to another. Everywhere the transmission of life, not the creation of life. And so when a man becomes good, what is it? Not a spontaneous generation, not a sheer leaping up of flame as if there had never been any fire in the universe before, *but* a transmission of the eternal goodness, a repetition of that which took place in the body when, in the mysterious words of Genesis, God breathed into man's nostrils the breath of life and man became a living soul. . . . The picture of what Christ does for us in our salvation is before us, all the time, in what men do for one another. . . . Christ gives us His life. You cannot give another what you have not yourself. Christ gives his life to us, and that is the way in which we come to live.

"So long as we see men give themselves to one another, and the power of one man passes into another man's life, so long it cannot be unintelligible or incredible that Christ gives Himself to us. So long as one illuminated object casts light on another, so long I can believe that the sun casts his light upon them all. You cannot put power into the wheel you turn, that is not first in the arm with which you turn it. You cannot put beauty into the house you build, that is not first in the soul with which you plan it. And so in St. Paul's doctrine, rightly understood, it is Christ's righteousness which clothes the righteous soul here, and in which it stands, happy and pure and meritless, at last. '*He that hath the Son hath life.*'"

That Phillips Brooks attached supreme importance to this answer to the question, What shall I do that I may enter into life, is shown most clearly and with the deepest pathos in this circumstance that, in the last sermon which he wrote, he took again for his text, "I am come that they might have life, and that they might have it more abundantly." He wrote the sermon as his farewell to Harvard College, and it was preached for the first and the last time in this pulpit. In this sermon he gathered up the experience of his life, offering it as his most precious legacy to the new class that was entering Harvard in 1891. Let me quote a few sentences from this sermon : —

"Among the words of Jesus, I do not know where we shall find larger words than these. They are very primitive and fundamental. They go back to the very beginning and purpose of His presence on the earth. What art thou here for, O wonderful, mysterious, and bewildering Christ? I am here that men may have life more and more abundantly. Could words go further back than this? Behind all special things which He wanted men to do and to be, behind all the great lessons which He wanted men to learn, He wanted men first of all to live. They are the words of a creator. It is that craving of life to utter itself in life which makes the beauty and the glory of the universe. He who speaks these words is very brave. He recognizes that the danger of men is not in too much life, but in too little. It is deficient vitality, not excessive vitality, which makes the mischief and trouble of the world. . . . Of course we know that Life is undefinable. No power of language has ever yet gathered up its vastness and its mystery into a compact and portable phrase. . . . If we may not define life in its essence, we may certainly recognize it in its results. Life is effectiveness. . . . When life enters into a man, his power of doing something, which no other man that lived could ever do, becomes a reality in the world.

"In every circle or community where you have ever lived, has there not been some man whom you knew as the life-giver? He was not perhaps the wisest man,

... he may not have been a learned man, ... but he *increased vitality.* He caused men to do their best. He quickened languid natures. ... Such men there are in history. ... Such a man I doubt not there is in the little group that makes your world. When we have realized such a man as that, and seen just what he is in the great world, then we have come where we can understand Christ, and seen just what was the meaning of his self-description.

"Sometimes people count up Christ's acts, and stand with the little group of jewels in their open hands, looking at them with something like puzzled wonder, and saying, 'Is this, then, all that He did?' Other people gather Christ's words together, and feel, through all their marvelous beauty, a bewildering sense that they do not account for the marvelous power of His life. But sometimes there comes a truer apprehension. The things He did, the things He said, were only signs and indications of what He was. He was not primarily the Deed-doer or the Word-sayer. He was the Life-giver. Wherever He went He brought vitality, ... creating the conditions in which all sorts of men should live. ... Everywhere this was true, men *lived by Him.* 'Ye will not come unto me, that ye might have life,' was his cry of bitter disappointment. 'He that eateth me, the same shall live by me,' was His consummate definition of His power. At the head of all life-givers stands the Life-giving Son of Man."

Such was the personality of Christ as it was given to Phillips Brooks to conceive and portray it. But his vision of Christ carried him further. It was essential to know whence Christ derived His life in order to enter fully into the secret of his power. The personality of Christ had its source and its deepest root in God. Words like these were constantly on the lips of Christ: I came not to do mine own will, but the will of Him that sent me. When still a boy in the temple He had learned this truth: Wist ye not that I must be about my Father's business? And again: As my Father hath taught me, I speak these things, and He that sent me is with me; the Father hath not left me alone; for I do always those things that please Him. When Jesus had said these words, so runs the sacred narrative, many believed on Him.

Here is a picture from the gospel narrative which tells the whole story as in an epitome. The place where it is written is the Gospel according to St. Matthew, the 22d chapter and the 34th verse: "But when the Pharisees had heard how that Jesus had put the Sadducees to silence, they were gathered together. Then one of them, which was a lawyer, asked Him a question, tempting Him, and saying, Master, which is the great commandment of the law? Jesus said unto him,

Thou shalt love the Lord thy God with all thy heart, and with all thy soul, and with all thy mind. This is the great and first commandment."

Surely it needs no other words to confirm this statement that Jesus attributed the source of personality to God. "As the Father hath life in Himself, so hath He given unto the Son to have life in Himself." The first and the great commandment sends every man to God who seeks the highest for himself or for others. I may not enter here upon many lines of thought which these words suggest. In the first and great commandment lies the warrant of all self-culture, the consecration of all human research and inquiry, the richest traits of human development, all that the world holds most dear and precious, — individual freedom, the power of personality. In the love of God with all the heart, and all the mind, and all the strength lies the guarantee of modern civilization as well. The tyrannies which beset us to-day, or those recorded in history, have sprung up because men have for a time failed in their love of God. We can put our finger on the weakest spot in our modern life when we test it by the first and great commandment. If individual liberty is to-day endangered, it is because our sense of loyalty to God is not as strong as it ought to be.

But I turn away from these considerations to the method by which each soul must come into contact with Christ in order to the transmission of eternal life. In the minds of many, there is vagueness and uncertainty as to what the highest is; and, if it has been recognized, there is a difficulty felt as to what is the exact thing to do when Christ calls to us, "Come unto me; I am the way, and the truth, and the life." Let me answer again in the words of Phillips Brooks, from this last sermon which he preached at Harvard:—

"All life is God's life. This is Christ's splendid doctrine of the Fatherhood of God. He realized it first in Himself. He was the Son of God; *His* life was God's life. . . . He would put the Child into the Fatherhood. 'No man cometh unto the Father but by me. He that hath seen me hath seen the Father.' This setting of the less finite into the complete infinite, Christ calls by various names. Sometimes it is *faith*, you must believe in God. Sometimes it is *affection*, you must love God. Always what it means is the same thing, you must *belong* to God. . . . Sometimes he seems to gather up His fullest declaration of this vital connection of man with God and call it in one mighty word *obedience*. You must *obey* God, and so live by Him. How words degrade themselves! . . . This great word ' obedience ' has grown base and hard and servile. Men dread the thought of it as a disgrace. They refuse to obey, as if they were thereby asserting their dignity. In reality they are asserting their own weakness. He who obeys nothing receives nothing. Rather let us glorify obedience. It is not slavery but mastery. He who obeys is *master* of the master whom he serves. He has his hands in the very depth of his Lord's treasures. When God says to His people, Do this and live, He is not making a bargain; He is declaring a necessary truth, He is pronouncing a necessity. He who does my will possesses *Me*. For my will is the broad avenue to the deepest chambers of my life. . . . 'Son, thou art ever with me, and all that I have is thine.' So speaks the infinite God to the obedient Child. . . . Obedience means mastery and wealth. Therefore let us glorify obedience, which is light and life, and dread disobedience, which is darkness and death."

When Phillips Brooks died in 1893, many attempts were made to estimate his rare and wonderful endowments. The question was asked as to his place in history. Would his fame endure? Would coming ages hold him to be as great as he had appeared to be in his own generation? How did he compare with other great men in the past? And more particularly men asked as to the degree and quality of his intellectual capacity. Was he a scholar, a profound thinker? Was he deeply read in philosophy or in the learning of the schools? All admitted the phenomenal character of his career. Nothing like it had been known before in this generation for the manifestation of a world-wide power, as intense also as it was wide in its range. But we failed to classify him as a thinker or as a scholar. It was not as these that he triumphed. It seemed as though his intellect was profound and subtle and vast also in its range of comprehension. But his appeal to his generation was not wholly an intellectual one. He offered no new philosophy; he criticised no dogmas; he urged no new beliefs; he had no theory to offer for the solution of the world's problems. He had indeed so much intellectual appreciation and insight, combined with the charm of the poetic imagination, that we wondered and admired; but when we analyzed, we failed to reproduce the combination that made him great.

The real secret of his greatness did not lie in these directions. It was in the power of his will. He defined life, he viewed life, as having its essential quality in the will. All other things came back to that. The will to live, that constituted manhood, as it was also the principle running through all the grades of the creation. This gift of a mighty and almost irresistible will was in him by inheritance, the concentrated inheritance of a long line of Puritan ancestors. Herein lay the essence of the Puritan theology, that it conceived of God as will, as sovereign will. This was the motive of the Puritan movement in all its stages, a desire to enforce what was believed to be the will of God. This was its watchword and its battle-cry in the storms of revolution in the English civil war. This led the Puritans to America, — a great determination of the human will to enforce the divine will.

Phillips Brooks, then, came legitimately by his endowment and his conviction that the will was the supreme power in man to which all other things must minister, the knowledge and the experience of life, or the knowledge that came through books and learning. He was unlike most other men, in that he had little interest in ideas for their own sake. He searched for them, he was familiar with them; but he never tossed them over and turned them about, or reasoned regarding them. He could not sit down and calmly discuss opinions about things. He had an aversion to theories as such; he was never led into controversy, but shunned it with an innate repugnance. It was because his intellect only served him as it ministered to his will to live. His inner life was stormy and tumultuous, with something of the violence of the primeval elements in commotion. Every truth that he saw was a source of new excitement, until he had registered it in terms of the will. His mental process was a perpetual transmutation of intellectual truths, or convictions, or experiences, whether his own or others', into an appeal to the will. He searched in every direction for food to satisfy that insatiable appetite of the will to live. Life to him was one great unity. He did not separate the religious from the secular life. He did not sharply distinguish between religious duties and the duties of common life. The obedience called for in the university, or in the professions, the institutions or vocations of life, was a religious principle as much as prayer or worship. He knew only one distinction, — between good and bad, right and wrong. Life was the good and the right; all that ministered to these was religious and sacred wherever it might be found, in art or literature, philosophy or science. Whatever increased vitality was of divine origin. It was not things in themselves that were worldly or injurious, but the spirit or temper with which the world and the things that are in the world were followed. Worldliness was simply the absence of the love of God. He who loved God possessed the world in its fullness, and his life became ever more rich and full. Thus, as far as it was in his power, Phillips Brooks was a man of the world because he was first a man of God. He gave us therefore in himself the type of modern sainthood. It is consecration, not renunciation, which makes the highest character. That was the principle embodied in his life. As the years went on, we came to admire and reverence the man, and to recognize that his eloquence and his power proceeded from his life. This was something very rare, very beautiful, that in one so richly endowed, with such a wonderful career, men should stand in awe of his personality as his greatest achievement.

In a private letter, which I have had the

privilege of reading, we are allowed for a moment to look directly into his own soul. The letter was written in the last years of his life, not long before the end : —

"Most surely these latter years have had a peace and fullness which there did not use to be. I say it in deep reverence and humility. I do not think that it is the mere quietness of advancing age. I am sure it is not indifference to anything I used to care for. I am sure that it is a deeper knowledge and a truer love of Christ. And it seems to me impossible that this should have come in any way except by the deepening experience of life. . . . All experience comes to be but more and more pressure of His life on ours. It cannot come by one flash of light, or one great convulsive event. It comes without haste and without rest in the perpetual living of our life with Him. And all the history of outer or of inner life, or the changes of circumstances or the changes of thought, gets its meaning and value from this constantly growing relationship to Christ. I cannot tell you how personal this grows to me. He is here, He knows me and I know Him. It is no figure of speech. It is the reallest thing in the world, and one wonders with delight what it will grow to as the years go on."

There are other aspects of Phillips Brooks' teaching and of his conception of the influence of Jesus[1] which must here be passed

[1] Cf. his treatise entitled, *The Influence of Jesus*, published by E. P. Dutton and Co., New York.

over for want of time or as not directly related to my theme. The subject which has been assigned for this lecture, — the Message of Christ to the Individual, — I have treated in a concrete way, by dwelling upon Phillips Brooks, not only as a preacher but as a man, who first received and embodied the message in his life, before he urged it, with the power of his own personality, upon other men. In the further fulfillment of my task let me turn to speak of him in whose honor, and for whose sacred memorial, this new lectureship is founded.

William Belden Noble was a graduate of Harvard in the class of 1885. As he appeared to his contemporaries in college, he was a man of beautiful and winning presence, marked by earnestness and enthusiasm, by directness of manner and of purpose, by unaffected genuineness and sincerity. He exhibited a sane and healthy nature, the foe of shams, — a thoroughly wholesome spirit, whom to know was to love. He was faithful as a student, with a wistful earnestness for the best and highest. His peculiar intellectual gifts seemed at first to lie in the direction of the natural sciences. He was eager in the acquisition of scientific facts, not as intellectual curiosities but as parts of a larger whole. He had a strong intuitive grasp of mathematical truth. He had another characteristic, which is the stamp of a Harvard man, — the open mind and the love of the truth : truth for its own sake was with him a consuming passion. But he was also known in college for his devotion to athletics. It was almost with a reckless abandon that he threw himself into college sports. In his freshman year he was on the football team; he played baseball with great success; he was interested in lacrosse, becoming captain of the team in his junior year; and, in addition to this, was a master of tennis, — a game which was then developing. He had his theories as to rackets and courts and balls and all the rules of the game; and whatever he went into in the line of athletics, he did it with his whole heart and intelligence. It was one of his theories that the sound body thus gained was indispensable to the sane mind. He cultivated sports as a means of enabling him to do better intellectual work. As he went on in college life, his love for the natural sciences seemed to yield to another interest, the study of English literature, for which there was then a growing enthusiasm. He had further the gift of speech, the happy knack, in making an address, to say the right thing at the right time.

Such he was, as he appeared to his fellow-students. But college men may fail to know each other, through conventionalities that conceal their interior life from easy or careless observation. There were in him other motives, and an inward experience, a sacred ideal for himself, known only to his intimate friends. He felt the charm and the beauty of life. Born as he was to the inheritance of wealth, he had been able to gratify his love for the beautiful in the study of art, and, by extensive foreign travel, to enrich his mind. He had a passionate love of nature. He first opened his eyes upon the world on the shores of Lake Champlain. The expansiveness of the Lake, lying open to the full vision of the sun, guarding no mystery or secret to be concealed, with the Green Mountains on the one side and the Adirondacks on the other, near enough to give sublimity, but not so near as to overshadow or darken;

with ever-changing visions of exquisite beauty corresponding to every change of position in the beholder, — such were the external aspects of nature with which he was familiar from his infancy, the objects of his latest love. Here in his last years he had built for himself a home, where all day long in the summer season he might live his outdoor life and revel in the beauty of sunrise and of sunset.

His artistic temperament, inherited from his gifted mother and developed by her teaching, commingled in organic fusion with deep moral purpose, the legacy of an upright, sturdy ancestry; his spiritual instincts, his quick aptitude for truth, his inborn love of goodness, — these all combined in creating the conviction that the true, the beautiful, and the good must have one common source, varieties of expression only for God as their essential reality. He interpreted beauty as the handwriting of God; he recognized in the loveliness of the landscape "a wayside sacrament," causing him to give thanks to the Giver of every good and perfect gift.

But he possessed another endowment in his love of moral beauty. With chivalry and courtesy and high dignity in his demeanor, with great gentleness and tenderness and sweetness of spirit, yet was he also uncompromising in his devotion to what was right. He had adopted the maxim that "questions of right and wrong had neither time nor place nor expediency." This moral capital was in part his inheritance from forefathers near and remote, a mantle worn more gracefully because it came to him by no effort of his own; yet had he also improved the talent of native goodness by putting it out at usury in the exchange of life. Thus to the instincts of his boyhood there was added in the years of youth the quick and glad response to whatsoever things are good, whatsoever things are pure, whatsoever things are true or honest, whatsoever things are lovely or of good report.

> "High nature amorous of the good,
> But touched with no ascetic gloom;
> And passion pure in snowy bloom,
> Through all the years of April blood."

Before he came to his full inheritance of religious faith, he passed through a period of doubt and misgiving. The religion of his boyhood was of that stern type which strengthened our Puritan ancestors with an almost superhuman courage, and inspired them for great deeds. If for no other reason, it should be spoken of with respect. Yet there were sides of life to which it did not minister. Whether or no the fault was inherent in the theology or in the religious cultus of the Puritan, or whether another age and new conditions of life created demands which it could not satisfy, I will not try to determine. But with him there was a struggle before he emerged into a new atmosphere, where the thought of God was the source of a deeper joy, and in the obedience of Christ as Lord and Master, no longer a servitude, but a service which was joy and perfect freedom. In this process of spiritual development he turned to the teachers who offered aid.

There was in him by nature something of the mystic, with whom the communion of the soul with God is deeper and more real than any of the incidents of the outward life. He possessed also something of the genius for the religious life. Among these teachers of experience was George Macdonald, with whom he had personal acquaintance, whose beautiful suggestions and subtle interpretations of the religious conventionalities, which had become threadbare by familiar usage, enabled many to make the transition, without injury or danger, from a type of religion against which the soul and reason was in revolt to a simpler, more rational faith, embracing and consecrating the whole life of man. Reverence as we must the spiritual earnestness in the leaders and representatives of Puritanism, yet, as Principal Tulloch has remarked, "are we also bound, if we would not empty our earthly existence of the beautiful and grand, the graceful, fascinating, and refined, in many forms of civilization and art, to claim admiration for much that they despised, and a broader, more tolerant, and more general interpretation of nature and life than they would have allowed."

The strongest religious influence came to him from Phillips Brooks. He listened to him on Sundays in his pulpit at Trinity Church; he followed him with vast admiration in his utterances at Harvard. He became, as did many others, his devoted disciple, sitting at his feet to learn the truth as it is in Jesus. From this time he entered more and more into the fuller possession of his manhood. His intense and eager appetite was finding its true food. His energy gained new avenues for expression. His fine qualities of heart and mind, palpitating with strong desire for assertion, were subjected to the Lordship of Christ. He had caught the secret of joy and of power, the new life which enabled all the functions of his buoyant manhood: it was, to bring every thought into captivity to the obedience of Christ. He threw himself with new vigor into the life of a college man in his day. He seemed to be absorbed in athletics as if he lived for them alone; he won his success in theatricals. He was fond of the Whist Club; for a time he took almost the sole charge of Memorial Hall. He was one of the editors of "The Crimson." He was a member of various college societies, the O. K., the Δ. K. E., the Institute, and the Hasty Pudding Club. He was fascinated with his work in English, punctiliously performing the requirements of the class-room. But beneath all this there flowed a deeper stream, which was the real current of his being. He was holding prayer meetings in his room, seeking to impart to others the joy in life which he had gained. More and more the thought grew upon him that it was his calling in life to minister to others, to become an agent for diffusing the power of that divine personality of Christ which had entered into and taken possession of his soul.

When he graduated, he was among those of the highest rank in his class, receiving honorable mention in English and English composition, and in political economy. The part assigned to him at Commencement was a Dissertation, for which he took the subject of Faith, — a fitting topic for one whose life and thought were guided by faith and consecrated to truth.

And now there came a change in his hitherto unbroken experience. The hand of disease was laid upon him. In his Senior year he had been obliged to leave college, and did not graduate with his class. After taking his degree in 1885, he entered the Episcopal Theological School to make direct preparation for the ministry, but at the end of a year's study he was again forced by ill-health to relinquish his work. Then followed years of struggle with the growing weakness which was undermining the powers of the body, years wherein his faith was put to the severest test. He was laid aside from active life to battle with depression and inward agony. He wandered here and there in search of health, spending much of his time abroad, but without gaining relief. He was forced to study life from another point of view, — to confront in all its aspects the problem of human suffering, and how it should be reconciled with the goodness and the love of God. But through all this trial, ever growing deeper and darker, he did not yield his faith in God. Instead of adopting the advice given to the typical sufferer in every age, " Curse God and die," he clung more closely to God. He stayed himself upon the thought of the Divine presence; he prayed for deliverance and for the power to endure; but the culmination and the focus of his prayer was always one petition, " *Make us conscious of thy presence.*" Unable as he was to undertake active service for others, limited and shut in when he was still eager and anxious to be of use in the world, he adopted one simple rule of guidance and consolation, — " Do the best you know how, and leave results with God." Other things that he said in the days of his trial reveal the depth of that faith which held him in its own possession: "What seems to us failure or catastrophe is fulfillment if Christ is ruling our lives," or again: "Hopes must not rule our lives, but truth and love, love to our wonderful God, and to our dear ones on earth."

He was forced to confront in the days of his youth the mystery of death, and its relation to life. In one of Drummond's tracts, which was among the last things he read, he marked the passage: —

"The condition necessary for the further evolution is that the spiritual be released from the natural. That is to say, the condition of the further evolution is Death. *Mors Janua Vitæ* therefore becomes a scientific formula. Death, being the final sifting of all correspondences, is the indispensable factor of the higher life. In the language of Science, not less than of Scripture, *To die is gain.*"

In the last year of his life he made one final supreme effort for the recovery of health and strength. It cost him an effort, which tore his soul with anguish, to go forth alone to the distant West in order to get the benefit of out-door life upon a ranch. Separated from his family, from wife and child, he brooded over the strangeness and the mystery of the ways of what he knew was an overruling Providence. But, deep as was the mystery, the consolations of God were with him, and they were not small. He was in the midst of glorious scenery, in a valley surrounded by mountains whose snow-peaks were pointing to God. Writing to his wife, he speaks of these things. As he was returning one evening, he had a lovely view down the valley, and spent the time, as his horse walked slowly along, in making to God a prayer and a thanksgiving. He prayed that the compulsory separation might be in some way a blessing, — " a good pray all in a lovely country." And again he wrote, and these were his last words: "I live in the ever-present consciousness of my God, so near, so loving, so great."

The end came suddenly, out-of-doors, as became a lover of nature, beside the clear, sparkling waters, fresh and pure like the river of the water of life, — a quick transition from the beautiful heart of nature into the great and new experience of the heart of God. He had asked life of God, and God gave him a long life, even forever and ever.

Such a life as this I have been describing,

when we contemplate it in the light of faith, is marked with the distinction of success and closes in victory. To human vision it may have seemed like defeat to be cut off in the midst of one's days, before an opportunity had been afforded to test the strength, or to reap the results of labor in the vineyard of God. The conventional symbols which express the human pathos are the broken shaft, the temple begun but left unfinished, the pitcher broken at the fountain. But does not such a life speak to us lessons of truth and of power? Was it not the typical human life, as God meant it to be? Had he not already entered into life through the power of Him who said, "I am come that they might have life, and that they might have it more abundantly"? Had he not eternal life in his possession, if the words of Jesus be recalled, "This is eternal life, to know Thee and Jesus Christ, whom thou hast sent"? Had not his faith in Christ whom he served been rewarded in the fulfillment of the promise, "I give unto them eternal life, and no one shall snatch them from my hands"? How far this eternal life, imparted to him, may have touched others in this world, it is not given to us to determine. All life is contagious, and " no man liveth unto himself, and no man dieth unto himself." He exerted his true influence, while he lived, upon all with whom he came in contact. In his sphere, however limited it may have been, he was an agent for the diffusion of life, of goodness and purity, beauty and truth.

> " To pass through life beloved as few are loved,
> To prove the joys of earth as few have proved,
> And still to keep the soul's white robe unstained, —
> Such is the victory he has gained."

*He, being made perfect, in a short time fulfilled a long time; for his soul pleased the Lord: therefore hasted He to take him away.*

It is one of the beneficent results of what we call death that it transfigures its object, to the imagination, as with the intensity of spiritual light, bringing out in clear relief the essential man in the true and most real purpose of his being, no longer obscured by the accidents of life. When she, whose privilege it was as his wife to receive this strong man's love, contemplated his transfiguration on the elevation of spiritual heights, she was filled with a longing that others might know the power of Christ as she had witnessed it in the illumination and consecration of a life. She turned to this University, where his happy years had been passed, offering her gift to constitute a perpetual foundation for making known the Influence of Jesus as the way, the truth, and the life. But it should be no restricted foundation; it should be as comprehensive as the range of the highest interests of man, — the consecration of the whole life by the spirit of purity, of truth, and of love. To her husband as to herself, Phillips Brooks had stood as an exponent, both in his character and in his preaching, of the life as it is in Jesus. To this was owing his universal sympathy, and the contagious appeal of his teaching to men of every class, and more particularly to young men on the threshold of life. Thus would she make her appeal to each generation of college men to turn to Jesus for life. So would she continue the work which her husband would have done, and help also to keep alive at Harvard the memory of its great son and greatest preacher, who loved the University as a part of his own being, who spent himself without stint in order to minister to its well-being.

I have been dwelling in this lecture on the duty of man to himself. The new age is preoccupied with the task of carrying out, as it has not been done hitherto, the duty of men to each other, — the second commandment of the law, Thou shalt love thy neighbor as thyself. For the better fulfillment of this task, has not Phillips Brooks prepared the way by dwelling upon the duty toward God, — the first and the great commandment? To perform rightly and successfully the duty toward man, it is the first requisite that we should recognize the value of the personality which is grounded in God. We must have some standard for self-love, and for self-cultivation, before the injunction to love our fellow-men as ourselves can have its perfect work. The standard for selfhood is to aim at the Divine fullness and perfection, — " Be ye perfect, as your Father which is in Heaven is perfect." We may fail in our duty toward others if we have not first striven to develop and enrich the personality of the individual man. There is such a thing as trying to minister to others when we are starving ourselves, — to feed the hungry when we ourselves have no food.

*Others have labored, and we have entered into their labors.*

*One man planteth, and another watereth, but God giveth the increase.*

*Every foundation endureth which is built upon Christ as the corner-stone.*

*All things come of thee, O Lord, and of thine own have we given Thee.*

May the blessing of God rest upon this new lectureship! May it serve to tie the generations together and in coming ages remind those that follow us of the truth which the nineteenth century has worked out in its representative preacher that "life eternal is to know God, and Jesus Christ whom He has sent." Let us praise God that He has put it into the heart of the founder to make the gift for its establishment. May His blessing rest upon her, giving her the fruition of her hopes and prayers, her love and her tears!

Let us further, pray: — Almighty God, with whom do live the spirits of those who depart hence in the Lord, and with whom the souls of the faithful, after they are delivered from the burden of the flesh, are in joy and felicity, we give thee hearty thanks for the good examples of all those thy servants who, having finished their course in faith, do now rest from their labors. Especially these two, William Belden Noble and Phillips Brooks, do we commemorate before thee. And we beseech Thee that we, with them, may have our perfect consummation and bliss, both in body and soul, in thy eternal and everlasting glory, through Jesus Christ our Lord. Amen.

# II

## THE MESSAGE OF CHRIST TO HUMAN SOCIETY

By the Rev. FRANCIS G. PEABODY, D.D.

# THE MESSAGE OF CHRIST TO HUMAN SOCIETY

" For their sakes I sanctify myself." — JOHN XVII. 19.

IN the introductory lecture of the present series there were described the touching circumstances which have prompted this gift to the University, and the permanent memorial which the gift creates. Let me, therefore, as one associated with the University staff, begin this second lecture by expressing, in behalf of the University, the gratitude and hope with which it accepts this endowment. Among the most important English contributions made in our generation to theology and philosophy have been the volumes made possible by endowments similar to the William Belden Noble Lectureship. For more than a century the Bampton Lectures have been an important incident in the life of Oxford. For sixteen years, from 1878 to 1894, the Hibbard Lectureship, in London, has disseminated a more just and comprehensive view of the great religions of the world, and of the nature and authority of Christianity. For seven years since 1890, the Gifford Lectureship, in Scotland, has produced a series of important contributions to the philosophy of religion, and now, for the first time in the history of such British endowments, appoints two of its lecturers from the ranks of our own scholars. Yet it is not as a duplication of such endowments that this University accepts the present trust. The Noble Lectureship is specifically designed by its founder to perpetuate among us, not primarily a way of thinking, but a way of life. The gift is definitely associated with that name which to this generation and this University best represents the comprehensiveness, power, and beauty of the Christian life. It is to be administered, according to the terms of the gift, "in accordance with the large interpretation of the influence of Jesus by the late Phillips Brooks, with whose religious teaching both the founder of the lectures and he in whose memory the lectures were established were in deep sympathy."

The University welcomes this characteristic of the gift. Here, for seven years, as

Preacher to the University, Phillips Brooks lavished upon us the blessings of his eloquence and his faith. To any one who can recall those days, this chapel will ever be filled with the aroma of his teaching, the dignity of his mighty presence, and the irresistible and all-embracing message of his love. He found great happiness in this relationship, and both to those who had the privilege of association with him, and to the youth to whom he spoke, no other modern interpreter of the life of man has spoken with such authority. His abounding sense of the richness and potency of life swept through our academic world like the southerly breeze which calls out the life of spring. One cannot help thinking how he would welcome a gift to this University, whose scope — as the founder of this lectureship lays down — " shall be as wide as the highest interests of humanity," and in which, as she urges, " the consecration by the spirit of Jesus of every department of human character, thought, and activity may be included, as well as theology and the more direct interests of the religious life." In later years the Noble Lectures will no doubt have their place within the building which will commemorate among us the precious memory of Phillips Brooks; and within that building will be set a memorial of that young minister of Christ so early cut off from his desire for Christian service, whom the great bishop inspired and trained, and who, through many generations, will be associated with all the higher interests of our University life. It was, says the founder of the lectures, the supreme desire of her husband to make known the meaning of the words of Jesus: "I am come that they might have life, and might have it more abundantly." May God grant that this life-imparting quality may be perpetuated among us through the trust now committed to our charge; and that from year to year the life of the University may be touched afresh by the life of Jesus Christ, and we may have life, and life more abundantly.

Such is the sense of responsibility, and such the sacred memory, with which the University accepts this memorial gift. . Yet, as we thus recall the ministry of Phillips Brooks and its historic place, it becomes plain that, even in the few years which now lie between us and his preaching, a new aspect of Christian life and duty has come abruptly into the foreground of our thought. The work of Phillips Brooks seems to have been set at the end of one period in the religious history of this country, and at the beginning of a new epoch into which he did not fully and deliberately enter. His message was — as was said a week ago — the message of Christ to the individual soul. Personality, life, will, his biographer has told us, were the great words of his ministry. It was the old gospel of personal redemption and renewal set forth with new richness and beauty and joy. Phillips Brooks was not a social reformer or organizer; he was not a sociologist or an ecclesiastic. In the last year of his life, and just as he was assuming the office of bishop, he said one day: "I care less and less for machinery." His commanding appeal was to the individual, and his permanent monument is to be found, not in an institution or organization or movement, or even a church, but in the humbler, braver life of thousands of individual souls made known to themselves through him. But it cannot be denied that in these last few years we have come upon what must be called a new age in Christian history. A new aspect of the gospel of Christ claims attention, and a new form of Christian obligation calls for definition and for loyalty. This is the age of the social question. The most marked quality of the present time is the renaissance of social responsibility. The inquiry of students of Christianity to-day is, in an unprecedented degree, directed to the social teaching of Jesus Christ, and the bearing of the gospel on the troublous problems of poverty, industry, and social duty which beset the modern world. When one recalls those great words of Jesus which I have taken for my text, perhaps the greatest words which even He ever uttered, it seems as if the world had heard first one phrase and then the other of the whole. "I sanctify myself,"— that was the earlier message to the individual, the message of personal spiritual consecration. "For their sakes,"— that is the call of the present to works of mercy and service, a call so commanding to many a modern man that it almost makes him forget that he has a soul, or almost ashamed to be concerned for its sanctification. I need not point out what an extraordinary transition is here. It transfers the centre of human interest from the world within to the world without; from the problems of the individual to the problems of the common good; from introspection to activity; from the religion of personal salvation to a religion which repeats the Master's word: "He saved others, Himself He cannot save." The new spirit makes, in Canon Fremantle's phrase, "the world the object of redemption." History, philosophy, science, are precious for their bearing on social welfare. It is a mighty, generous, healthy-minded sweep of human interest out of all cloistered, isolated, self-centred consideration of the purpose of life into the brave, self-effacing service of the modern world. Such is the present age. Never before in human history were so many people, scholars and hand-workers alike, rich and poor, men and women, so profoundly impressed by inequalities of social conditions, by demands of social justice, by possibilities of social change, by dreams of social redemption. If, then, the Christian religion is to have any serious part in moulding the present age, it must be because of its peculiar and hitherto unrecognized applicability to these perplexing issues of the time. The earlier centuries have heard the solemn message of Christ to the individual; but now a new demand is laid upon the gospel, — to interpret and direct the unprecedented social tumult and desire of the modern world. What, then, has religion to say to these things? What is the social teaching of Jesus Christ? What is Christ's mission to human society? That, indeed, is a question much too searching to be adequately dealt with in an hour; but it is the question which in all branches of the Christian church, Catholic and Protestant alike, and in the mind of every thoughtful Christian who reads the signs of the times, is pressing for a reply.

The first thing, then, which one should note as he approaches the question, is the obvious fact that Jesus Christ was not primarily a social reformer, or the deviser of a social programme, or the forerunner of social agitation or revolt. No description of his mission could be less accurate than to identify it with the social arrangements or readjustments or revolutions which are now so eagerly urged. One of the most curious characteristics of Christian history is the appropriation by each age in succession of the person of Christ as though He were exclusively devoted to the special ideals of that age. It is, indeed, one proof of the wonderful many-sidedness of the character of Jesus that He can be thus claimed in turn by such various ways of thought. A period of theological development discovers a Christ who is supremely absorbed in defining his own person; a period of ecclesiastical development finds encouragement in a Christ whose special mission was the foundation of a church; and now, instead of Christ the theologian, or Christ the ecclesiastic, we have offered to us a Christ who is an agitator, a revolutionist, a labor leader, or, as He has been lately called, "Jesus, the demagogue."[1] Sometimes this new discovery of the nature of Christ takes the form of a philosophy of Christianity. The doctrine of Christ, it is said, was social rather than theological. "The rejection of his social ideal was the crucifixion He carried in his heart." "The Sermon on the Mount is the science of society;" "it is a treatise on political economy, it is a system of justice," and "industrial democracy would be the actual realization of Christianity."[2] Now, over against all this

[1] *Contemporary Review*, March, 1896.
[2] G. D. Herron, *The New Redemption*, pp. 30, 38, 41.

inclination to read the gospel as a socialist tract, or an attack on the rich, or a labor-reform programme, is to be set the elementary truth that social programmes, politics, reforms, and revolutions, whatever principles concerning them may be derived from the teaching of Jesus, were simply not the centre of interest to his mind and heart. It might be fairly argued that they could not be; that the historic circumstances and conditions of his life made these problems — in the form, at least, in which they appear in the complexity of modern life — as remote and impossible to Him as definite instruction would have been about the negro question, or states' rights, or civil service reform. But apart from the practical impossibility of such specific dealing is the equally obvious fact that the mind of Jesus was distinctly turned another way. He was supremely devoted to the special mission of spiritual regeneration. He desired to disclose the unrecognized and unappreciated relationship of the soul of man to the life of God. "This is the first and great commandment: Thou shalt love the Lord thy God." "This is life eternal, — to know thee, the only true God." "I came forth," He says, "from the Father, and am come into the world;" again, "I leave the world and go to the Father:" and his disciples answer, "Show us the Father, and it sufficeth us." Jesus, that is to say, was not a reformer, He was a revealer. He would permit nothing to divert Him from this mission. At the very outset of his ministry, the devil set before Him precisely this part of political and social leadership, and He said, "Get thee hence, tempter." It was a degenerate age in the Roman world, but He refused to counsel revolution. "Render to Cæsar," He said, "what is his.[1]" There was social injustice enough about Him to be righted, but when such a grievance was brought to Him He said, "Man, who made me a divider over you?" In short, his message to manhood was not of the mechanism of society, but of the character and capacity and destiny of the human soul. To transform the gospel of Christ into a teaching of social change is to ignore the fact that the mind of Christ was on an end which made him comparatively unconcerned

---

[1] Compare Shaler Mathews, *The Social Teaching of Jesus*, Macmillan, 1897, p. 202 ff. The whole argument of this notable book is most painstaking and convincing.

with social machinery or programmes. He was wrestling, not against flesh and blood, but against spiritual wickedness in heavenly places. He was not a social artisan, He was a spiritual power; and when this quality of his mission became quite clear to his contemporaries, many of those who wanted to get from Him, as men do now, some short cut to prosperity and liberty, slunk away from Him, and there was even a look of distrust among his immediate friends which made Him say to them, "Will ye also go away?" The practical applications of science in our day often lead to results which happen, as it were, on the way to the results intended. What is called a by-product is thrown off, or precipitated, or separated in obtaining the product sought. The by-product may be of itself of the utmost value, — may indeed be more precious than the object sought; but none the less it is discovered by the way. Such is the social teaching of Jesus. Whatever it is, it happens on the way to his essential and central teaching of the present and quickening life of God. The forms and rules of human society do not make the centre or secret of his gospel. They are the corollaries of the mighty proposition that this is God's world, and we are his children. They are the by-product issuing from his transcendent revelation of the purpose of God fulfilled in the sanctification of man. Out of the cardinal doctrine of the fatherhood of God flows whatever other commandment is of like nature to it concerning the brotherhood of man.

Such, I suppose, is the unmistakable quality and note which marks the teaching of Jesus. And yet — one hastens to say — such a teaching of the life of God in the soul of man cannot be without a bearing upon problems of social duty and social order. If it is a mistake to identify the mission of Christ with a programme of social change, it would be a still greater mistake to imagine that his message did not carry with it a doctrine of social change, or that such a doctrine is remote, or Oriental, or inapplicable, or outgrown. Jesus is, indeed, not a social system-maker; but He may be, none the less, in the most radical and invigorating way, the quickener of social life. When, on some sultry day, a fresh afternoon breeze sweeps over some suffering city, and pallid faces brighten, and the pillows of the sick grow cool, and the work of the world lies easier on its shoulders, — that is not an achievement of a system-maker, as though it were devised by some judicious weather-bureau supervising all; it is simply the movement of the compassionate life of God across the weary life of man. And yet it "makes over," as we say, the human system, and revives the capacity to live and to hope. So sweeps the breeze of Jesus over the weariness and hopelessness of the world, not to systematize its life, but to revive its life; not to originate a doctrinal system, but to restore a vital system; and many a perplexing problem and enfeebling disease of the modern social world is swept clean away by this tonic visitation of a new ideal. The fact is that, with a suggestiveness and reiteration which cannot be ignored, the Gospel does present, as issuing from this central appeal to the religious life of man, an ideal of society which anticipates in a most extraordinary degree the dreams and desires of the present age. More than a hundred times in the brief narrations of the gospels occurs the phrase, "the kingdom," "the kingdom of heaven," "the kingdom of God." For the coming of this kingdom Jesus looked and longed. It was the one thing to be desired; it was the hid treasure; it was the pearl of great price; it was the net which should gather in the good, and from which the bad should be cast away. What was this social dream of Jesus, and when was it to be fulfilled? No one, in the face of the many learned volumes which weigh the utterances of Jesus on this subject, can affirm that his teaching as to the kingdom is without obscurity, or that different aspects of it do not seem at different times to present themselves to his mind. But the prevailing judgment of scholars turns more and more to the definition of the kingdom as a social ideal of brotherhood and peace. Certainly it was not a political kingdom of which He spoke, for He repeatedly rejected such a perversion of his thought. Nor was it a kingdom which should be realized in some future age or world, though the hope of Judaism pointed that way, and the language of Jesus often utilizes the Hebrew imagery.[1] But Jesus, gathering into his message all this vague

---

[1] Matt. xxv. 31; Mark ix. 1. Compare Wendt, *Teaching of Jesus*, ii. 341; Beyschlag, *New Testament Theology*, p. 49; and especially Shaler Mathews, *op. cit.* chs. iii. and viii.

popular dream of a remote millennium, announced that the new world of righteousness and peace was potentially present and spiritually near. "The time is fulfilled," He says, "the kingdom is at hand;" "to-day is the scripture fulfilled in your ears;" "the kingdom is in your midst;" "he that hath ears to hear, let him hear." In a word, the kingdom of God to Jesus Christ is not a remote utopia, or a post-mortem millennium; it is his vision of what might happen now, if people would but enter into the spiritual inheritance and blessing which God is waiting to bestow. It was the leaven which could make a lump into a loaf. It was the spiritual brotherhood of the poor in spirit and of the pure in heart. The perfect social order was not to Him an ideal dream. It was potentially present as He spoke. He is anointed to bring in the acceptable year of the Lord. He has a mission to human society. The better social order would come of itself, if his mission to the individual soul could have its way. The kingdom of God, He says, is in your midst if you would only accept the terms it offers. Was ever, indeed, any reformer of the modern time more visionary or audacious, or apparently impracticable, than this young man from the hill-town of Nazareth, as He stands there in the midst of Roman domination and Hebrew tradition, proclaiming this unconquerable assurance of an earthly kingdom of a living God?

Yet, impressive as is this teaching of Jesus as to the possible social redemption, a further question leads us more deeply into his thought. What, we ask ourselves, is to be the means of this better human society? What is to bring to pass this organic commonwealth of social service, this unobserved and spiritual brotherhood, this fulfillment of the kingdom of God? To this question there might present themselves two possible replies. Social regeneration might proceed, on the one hand, from without, by schemes, association, legislation, or, in general, by organization; or, on the other hand, it might proceed from within, through personality, character, insight, consecration, or, in general, by inspiration. Indeed, here is the fundamental distinction in social methods. On the one hand is the creation of the better life by change of conditions; and on the other hand is the transformation of conditions by the power of the better life. No absolute issue can be forced between these two ways of social progress, — regeneration by organization, and regeneration by inspiration. Both have their place in any healthy social movement. Yet it is of profound importance to determine how these two methods stand related to each other; and it is perfectly evident where the attention of the present time chiefly turns. We find ourselves in an age devoted, as perhaps no era in history has ever been, to social regeneration by social organization. Never before probably were there such associated activities, such combinations of capital, such organizations of labor, such multiplicity of societies and committees, and meetings for the amelioration of social life. The hope of millions of handworkers for a more equitable division of the products of industry is very largely set today on such external change. By legislation, by new social programmes, by more complete organization of industry, there is to come, either suddenly or slowly, the better social world. What seems to such persons to obstruct the coming of the Kingdom is some fault of organization, — the condition of land-tenure, or the tradition of private ownership, or the overwhelming combinations of capital, or the inadequate combinations of labor; and when, as they believe, the change once comes to pass of which they dream, in outward conditions, then there will issue from the new organization the new and nobler social world. The Christian church partakes of the time-spirit. No congregation maintains its own self-respect to-day without an elaborate mechanism of giving and praying, working and playing, with its own wheels of organization meanwhile in contact with other wheels in other churches, until the whole world of Christendom shall be brought to keep time in its mechanism and strike at one moment the hours of Christian progress.

And who shall say that this great, comprehensive, generous time-spirit, which is sweeping us all into its organized life, is not a blessing? Who does not see how much courage and power enter into many a timid life when it is taken out of its solitude into the organization of a common cause? These combinations of industry with all their combativeness and indiscretions are, after all, the very basis of the amazing industrial development of the present age; and this organization of religion is disclosing to multitudes, for the first time, the dimensions and the possibilities of their common faith.

Yet how evident it is that such organization is but the mechanism, the medium, the channel through which human personality may more effectively work. Organization magnifies a hundredfold the power of the individual; it offers to him a scope and hearing and leverage on life such as never before was in his hands: but the utilization of this wonderful mechanism of the modern world is more than ever dependent upon the preparedness of the individual, and, without that personal fitness for the new task, social organization is either lifeless and impotent or the instrument of evil. "Personality," said Bunsen, "is the lever of history;" and the history of religion, with which he was specially concerned, is the most impressive illustration of his truth. The great religions of the world have not had their missionary effect through a scheme or organization; they have been the perpetuated influence of persons whose remote and perhaps idealized inspiration has transformed the very character and temperament of whole races of men. It is a very striking fact that the modern science of sociology — if, in its struggling beginnings at self-definition, it can be called as yet a science — has already passed in its short history from an emphasis on the life of the mass to an emphasis on the power of the individual. The first speculations which dared to call themselves sociological grew out of this new sense of organization in social life. The solidarity of society, its unity and interdependence beneath all forms of change, its analogy with biological processes in growth and decay, — these aspects of social life arrested attention, and for a time the province of sociology was found in interpreting the classic phrase, " the social organism." It was a fruitful analogy. It banished from philosophy the thought of an isolated personality, a self whose rights and duties could be independently analyzed. It reiterated in scientific form the Pauline teaching of the social body, that we are members one of another, and that the weakness or strength of each member affects the whole organic life. Yet this biological analogy soon found its limitation. The law of social progress could not long be studied in modern life without coming upon the determining and transforming effect on the social mass which proceeds from a power without analogy in the organisms of nature, — the power of personality. Over against the biological conception of social life has been set the psychological interpretation, and it has been observed that modifications of social structure were in very large degree effected, not by growth of the organism, but by the originative impulse of the individual. Progress, it is pointed out, proceeds chiefly from imitation, — the impulse being given by the invention or vision or example of the master, and the mass of men induced to imitative acceptance or loyalty.[1]

Now precisely here, and with a force which no former age in history could adequately appreciate, enters the message of Christ to human society. Here are these two elements of progress, the mass and the person, the social organism and the social originator, regeneration by organization, and regeneration by inspiration, both of them essential, each waiting on the other's strength; and one asks,

[1] Consult *Polit. Science Quarterly*, xii. 430, for a summary of the doctrine of G. Tarde, *Lois de l'imitation*, 1895.

"Where, in this twofold problem, does the social teaching of Jesus Christ have its place?" Certainly, one must reply, He cannot be regarded as an expert adviser in social organization. His ministry simply antedated the complexity of modern life. Of one group alone, and that the most elementary, the family, does He speak with a positive doctrine and lay down a structural law. It is nothing but misdirected literalism to use the New Testament as a text-book of social structure. It is simply impossible to order modern life after the model of New Testament texts. This is a new world, with dimensions, unity, risks, problems, and possibilities inconceivable to an earlier age. Indeed, it is this unanticipated and unprecedented modern world itself which has created the organization which now it has to direct and control. But on the other hand, and with a discernment which makes the message of Jesus Christ modern and timely in a most dramatic degree, He turns to that factor of progress which, the more social organization is elaborated, is the more urgently needed. He habitually directs his message to the inspiration of individuals. He saves men one at a time. The shepherd seeks the one sheep; the woman sweeps the house for the one piece of money; the whole world may be gained, and it shall be valueless if a man forfeits his own soul. One of the most extraordinary traits of the ministry of Jesus Christ is his indifference to numbers. He sends the multitudes away. He is transfigured before two disciples. He speaks his profoundest words to one ignorant woman. The first gift of Christianity to human society is its recognition of an unappreciated and inestimable preciousness in each humblest human soul. How beautifully this is summed up by Phillips Brooks himself in his least read book, and in almost the only passage where he deals systematically with the social teaching of Jesus. "Jesus," says Dr. Brooks, "begins with the individual. He always does. Before all social life there is the personal consciousness and its mysterious private relations to the Father from whom it came." "The final unit is the man; and that unit of value was never out of the soul of Jesus." "After the day when He told them the story of the hundred sheep, and how the shepherd left all the rest and came down the hill singing with the rescued sheep across his shoulders, — after that keynote of the preciousness of the individual had been struck, it never ceased to be heard through everything that Jesus said and did." [1]

Thus the great preacher reiterates his Master's fundamental message. But why is it, we go on to ask, that this summons to the individual is the unit of the gospel teaching? For what end is the individual thus absolutely precious? For its own sake? Oh, no! Taken by itself, a human life cannot be regarded as of such tremendous significance. But Jesus is interpreting the single soul in the light of his universal kingdom. What He is looking for is not a self-acting social mechanism, but a source of power which can run through whatever mechanism the world provides, and make it leap into effectiveness; and this source of power He discovers in the individual life inspired by Him. It is as if the network of tracks and cars and wires in our city streets were all prepared for service and waiting for the power to utilize them; and as if, in some remote seclusion of the city's life, the power

[1] Phillips Brooks, *The Influence of Jesus*, 1878, p. 112 ff.

were generated, and silently and mysteriously went coursing along the wires to give life and meaning to the intricate whole. So, in the teaching of Jesus Christ, stands the individual in the midst of the social order. The organization of society is a problem which each age has to work out for itself; but the inspiration of society proceeds from the introduction into any form of social mechanism of the power of that life which is hid with Christ in God. No mechanical or external change can supplant this social dynamic. It is in vain to try to make a better world except by the antecedent creation of consecrated people. "There is no political alchemy," Mr. Spencer has said, "by which you can get golden conduct out of leaden instincts;" and many a scheme for social redemption has had its day, and ceased to be, because, with all its mechanical completeness, it failed of the power which could make it go. The whole creation groaned and travailed in pain, and finally was smitten with death, while it waited for the manifestation of the sons of God.

Such, it seems to me, is the attitude of Jesus toward the problems of the social world;

and we have here the reason why so few explicit utterances come from Him as to the machinery of social reform. It is not that He is indifferent to social welfare, for his hope and prayer were ever for his Father's kingdom; but it is that He discriminates between form and spirit, between mechanism and motive power, between organization and inspiration, and gives the whole mighty impulse of his teaching to the generating of the force which alone can transform and move and illuminate the social world. One of the most interesting aspects of Christian history is the rise or revival, at different points and periods, of the spirit of philanthropy, as if some new demand for expression was felt by the instinct of social service. Such an efflorescence of pity and sympathy marked, for instance, the beginning of Christianity itself, so that the revolution effected in the Roman world was hardly less one in humane and fraternal feeling than in religious ideals. Such renewals have often occurred in later times. England was quickened to such philanthropy forty years ago, and a great series of social movements, of coöperation, trade unions, and friendly societies began : the city of Boston was the scene of a similar awakening fifty years ago, and its judicious care of the poor, the blind, the insane, and the feeble-minded has been the pride of the city ever since : and now, in these last few years, another renaissance of social responsibility is felt in this country, and is illustrated in an unprecedented degree within our own college life. But when we look for the special impulses of these successive waves of philanthropy, we discover, strangely enough, that they have proceeded, not from agitators, or workers, or system-makers, but from preachers, prophets, seers. The beginnings of the English movement proceeded from the personality of Frederic Maurice; the earlier Boston philanthropy took its rise from the spiritual influence of William Ellery Channing; the new social service owes its central inspiration to the preaching of Phillips Brooks. Not one of these was an organizer of schemes, but each of them was a quickener of life; and the regeneration by organization fell to those who were stirred by the message of inspiration. It was the same with the influence of Jesus Christ. He did not organize philanthropy; but, none the less, out of his ministry came an absolutely new philanthropy. He gave what the world needs more than social service, — social courage. He sanctified people themselves, and then they were eager to live for others' sakes.

And, if this discernment of the source of power was possible in the time of Jesus, how much more justified and significant is it under the conditions of the modern world! Here is a time when the organization of industrial and social life has become complex and omnipresent beyond any parallel in history. It is an age which, superficially considered, seems to be controlled by masses of men, — by parties, democracies, majorities, unions, leagues; but beneath this external organization there is an opportunity for leadership, which makes of the consolidated mass such a weapon as the individual never had before. Precisely, then, because of its enormous complexity of organization, the modern world calls all the more for regeneration through inspiration. The more one recognizes the proportions of its mass-life, the more pressing becomes the demand for a new kind of person to direct these mighty forces.

It is like one of our great battleships, with all its complex arrangements of destructive and protective forces, yet with the control of the whole led up into that conning-tower where the individual has under his hand the whole vast, intricate machine. Thus, in the midst of the modern world stands the message of Christ to human society. "For their sakes," says the modern spirit, looking out to all the need and distress and social problems of the time, — "for their sakes" let us organize and legislate, and appoint sub-committees, and develop this machinery of relief. And to this the gospel of Christ answers, "It is well." Lay down these tracks of progress; devise this intricate mechanism through which sympathy may swiftly speed. But what shall make such mechanism live, except it become the channel of a wise and personal love? "For their sakes" then, says Jesus Christ, first of all, sanctify yourselves. First be fit to serve, and then serve for others' sakes. First life, then love. The social teaching of Jesus is a doctrine, not of methods of redemption, but of the capacity for redemption. There may be in theology a scheme of salvation, but in sociology there is no salvation by a scheme. The only salvation must be by saviors, and saviors are people who have sanctified themselves for others' sakes.

Such, most imperfectly and hastily, seems to be some indication of the message of Christ to human society. I said at the outset that it was a message which no former age had been called upon to hear, and which had come to us in the new exigencies of the present time. I said that into this new aspect of Christian thought Phillips Brooks was not called consciously to enter. And yet the message of Christ to society turns out to be at its heart no other than his message to the individual. The social regeneration of the world is to arrive, says Jesus, not through organization alone, and not through inspiration alone, but by the application to organization of the personal power inspired by Jesus Christ. The effective service "for their sakes" is to issue from those who have sanctified themselves. The mechanism of society waits to be utilized by the Christian spirit. The message preached by Phillips Brooks to the individual is not only the old gospel; it is at the heart of the gospel for to-day.

We look in one closing moment into the puzzling and baffling problems of the time, and we find them waiting thus for this message of Christ. Here is our modern charity, organized, systematized, scientific as never before; and Jesus gives us no instruction as to our committees or offices or machinery of relief. But into the heart of every charity administrator He looks and says: "See to it that your organization is a channel for the essential sympathy and humanity of man, and not a barrier against it." Organization may be but officialism, machinery, automatism. It may deal with a soul under the name of a "case," and its work may be so wooden as to be fitly called a "bureau." Beware of organization without inspiration. It is the body without a spirit, — a dead form and a hollow sham. But on the other hand here is this modern development of organization ready to make effective your personal help. It is the guarded, lighted road along which, for the first time in history, pity can walk securely, swiftly, and straight. Utilize it, says the Christian gospel. Multiply your power by such mechanism; the person who rejects these safeguards is simply not primarily concerned with the proper end of charity, the creation of personality, but his end is selfish emotion and comfortable self-deceit. He thinks himself full of pity, when he is really both indolent and cruel. His alms are a substitute for his conscience. The mechanism of relief stands ready for the will of the reliever, and never was there such scope for effective sympathy and wise kind-heartedness as is now provided for those who, through the organization of modern charity, sanctify themselves "for their sakes."

Or we turn to the still more perplexing issues of industry and the programmes of social change which are so hotly debated in our time, and we ask for the message of Jesus Christ to the trades-unionist and the employer, to the socialist and revolutionist of the time. Is he an agitator or organizer, with his own programmes of communism or anti-capitalism or reform? "Man," He answers, "who made me a judge or a divider over you?" The organization of industry is the problem of the modern age. But does this mean that the Christian religion stands neutral among these absorbing issues? On the contrary, it touches the very nerve of the social question, and discloses the very secret of effective and permanent organization. So act, says the Christian law, that organization shall quicken personality. The excellence of trade-organization lies in this, that it may vastly contribute to the liberty, intelligence, and manhood of the workers of to-day; and the peril of trade-organization lies in this, that it may limit or suppress the range of productive power or personal initiative or human sympathy. The ideals of socialism, which anticipate a commonwealth of equity and opportunity, are not only consistent with the social teaching of Jesus Christ, they are identical with it; but the schemes of socialism which devise a dictatorial rule under the form of democracy, and which forbid individual initiative under the form of liberty, these are not only inconsistent with the Christian ideal, but are in absolute and undisguised conflict with it. Beware then, says the teaching of Jesus Christ, of that economic programme which proposes regeneration by organization. Nothing could be more contrary to the spirit of Christ than the vain hope that changes in conditions of ownership will bring with them a change in the human heart. But enter, says the Christian teaching, into every movement of that moral socialism which obtains for the individual a fairer chance for human life among the dehumanizing conditions of the time. The vast organization of industry waits to-day for its utilization by Christian manhood. Never was there such a chance as the industrial world to-day presents for men of wisdom, insight, humanity, self-control, and sympathy, and never — though many a business man would mock at the thought — never, probably, such a reward. The mechanism of industry, the great dull grim giant of traffic and trade, is toiling on with downward look, like St. Christopher at his ferrying; but some day it will look up from the faithful fulfillment of its almost overwhelming task, and will see that the Lord Christ stands on the bank before it, and will know that to it has been intrusted the holy office of bearing the spirit of the Master through the turbulent stream of the present age.

Thus we look out from the quiet of the academic life and hear the message of Christ to these larger interests of poverty and trade; and then, last of all, the same message comes, and comes with a special clearness, to this special form of social order in which we are personally placed, — the microcosm of the college world. Here, as in all the world about us, there is an ever-increasing complexity of organization; and the simplicity of college life has expanded into university ideals, and the individual seems almost lost in the movement of the mass. A youth comes to our gates and a bewildering mechanism of study and opportunity confronts him, and he asks himself: "How can I enter into this whirling machine and be anything more than a cog among its wheels, without independence or initiative or soul of my own?" That is the first aspect of this great movement of academic life. Yet who that has any experience here does not know that never in the history of the college was there such an appeal to manhood, or such a chance for leverage for the individual on the mass, as there is now? Never before among us did the person, the right-minded, self-effacing, modest, manly man, have such a power for good. The very development of organization in university life enlarges the opportunity for leadership. Year after year we see the temper and tone of this great institution purified and sweetened by persons who have not the least idea of posing as social saviors, but who simply sanctify themselves for others' sakes. The cleansing of academic life is like the purifying of the great reservoir from which the city drinks. The wise engineer seeks the sources of supply, cleanses each pasture-bank, each trickling brook; and out of the purified life of the modest, unassuming sources the health of the great city is insured. One asks himself, then, as he sees this way of our social life, Suppose that, in our university world, the two factors of progress could fairly and fully meet; suppose that through our highly organized life there could flow with increased fullness the current of consecrated personal life; suppose that our work, our play, our companionship, could be not only mechanically excellent, but spiritually noble; suppose that here at the heart of the University this chapel, with its uncompelling invitation, with its open door for whosoever will, could from year to year establish even a few young souls in unassuming consecration, — then what might happen? Why, that would be, in this microcosm of social life, the coming of the kingdom of God; the mission of Christ to human society would be in one little corner of the great world fulfilled; and through the broad channel of our associated life would flow out from the heart of single souls the stream of personal service, singing as it flows: "I am come that others may have my life, and have it more abundantly." Even so near to us is the kingdom for which we daily pray. The kingdom of God, the potential reign of consecrated souls, says Jesus, is even now in your midst; and, out of the hopes and needs and mighty desire for the coming of that kingdom in this place we love, we answer, "Even so, Lord Jesus, come quickly."

# III

## THE MESSAGE OF CHRIST TO THE WILL

By the Rev. THEODORE T. MUNGER, D.D.

"Temptations in the wilderness! Have we not all to be tried with such? . . . Our Life is compassed round with Necessity; yet is the meaning of Life itself no other than Freedom, than Voluntary Force: thus have we a warfare; in the beginning, especially, a hard-fought battle. For the God-given mandate, *Work* thou in Welldoing, lies mysteriously written, in Promethean Prophetic Characters, in our hearts; and leaves us no rest, night or day, till it be deciphered and obeyed; till it burn forth, in our conduct, a visible, acted Gospel of Freedom. . . . To me nothing seems more natural than that the Son of Man, when such God-given mandate first prophetically stirs within him, and the Clay must now be vanquished or vanquish, — should be carried of the spirit into grim Solitudes, and there fronting the Tempter do grimmest battle with him; defiantly setting him at naught, till he yield and fly. Name it as we choose: with or without visible Devil, whether in the natural Desert of rocks and sands, or in the populous moral Desert of selfishness and baseness, — to such Temptation are we all called. Unhappy if we are not." — *Sartor Resartus*, ch. ix.

# THE MESSAGE OF CHRIST TO THE WILL

THE TEMPTATION IN THE WILDERNESS.
ST. MATTHEW IV. 1–12.

I TRUST that the title of my discourse will not lead any one to think that I am about to discuss the nature of the will. However it may have been in the past, there is to-day little need of such discussion. It confuses every-day thought on a point concerning which no one ever has a real doubt. There may be now and then a vagrant mind who indulges too freely in metaphysics, and persuades himself that the will is not free, or but partly free, with the possible result of some lapse in ethics, but none whatever in the instinct of self-preservation, or any other action requisite to his stay in the world. But these exceptions do not sensibly lessen the great majority who are equally conscious of freedom and personality, — one carrying the other. Dr. Johnson showed the absoluteness of his common sense in his remark: "The will is free; we know it, and that is the end of it."

Modern thought, if I may venture to speak for it, has ended the debate of ages by assuming, not that man has a will, but that he is a will; it is the will that makes him man, and of course it is free, or man is a very different being from what he takes himself to be.

I assume the will as the constituting feature of man; and I contend that a properly trained will is the basis and badge of true manhood.

I will not endeavor to show that the movement of human society is towards an ethical end. Evolution has settled that question. Nor will I waste a moment in efforts to prove that, while this process is going on through a Power not ourselves, we also have a part in the movement. Metaphysics may drive us up and down in this much-tossed sea of contradiction; but again we appeal to consciousness and to the daily habit of our lives, — the play of personal power among cosmical forces, inexplicable but a fact. The movement of society is by eternal law; it is also by the will of man. And because the end is ethical, the will that strives for the end must be ethical; it must be trained in ethics; it must be environed and buttressed by ethics; it must be made and kept strong by an assimilation of all those faculties and qualities in our nature that go to feed strength. Regarding the will as the central and constituting factor in man, all tastes, desires, aptitudes, capacities are to be looked at as so many servitors that stand about the will to nourish and guide it along right lines and to right ends. It is itself mere force, — blind and without purpose until these servitors come to their places about it.

Hence I speak of a trained will, and more particularly of an ethically trained will. In order to make a proper study of this subject we must go to the world of human life, — real life in a real world, and the more real the better for our purpose. To this end I direct your attention to that unique example whose name and person are enshrined in the Christian religion. I will take one phase or experience of that life, and endeavor so to speak of it that you can catch some glimpse, at least, of why it was and how it was that He became not only the greatest moral force that has yet appeared on this planet, but seems to be one with that other Force which is bearing the world surely and irresistibly on to its moral goal.

The experience I have in mind is that called the Temptation in the Wilderness.

The sources of Christ's moral consciousness previous to the Temptation may not easily be named; but if much is to be assigned to Jewish history and the Prophets, far more is to be ascribed to the play of his own nature. He was not the product of history nor of prophetism, but of the Spirit of God. And what was this in his case? A brooding of the Spirit over his conception and birth; a childhood haunted by the Spirit; a life possessed and directed by the Spirit into all true ways of thought and conduct, — so possessed that the secrets of his own nature became clear to him, and He knew who He was, and whence He came, and whither He would go. But Christ's consciousness did not stop here; it deepened and ripened into a sense of the Fatherhood of God, and along with it into a sense of Sonship. Which rose first? Let us not inquire; they represent an eternal and indefinable order. Fatherhood and Sonship played back and forth, each deepening the other until they had mastered his being. The two — developed under the realities of life — create the sum of human duties. A divine Father means a divine Son; and He will be a Son by perfect obedience. How else can He be a Son? The Spirit brooded over him continually, fluttering like a dove above his head but entering into his soul like a flame of fire. Fatherhood, Sonship, — here are the two poles between which human life realizes itself and its duties. A chief characteristic of the Hebrew nation was its capacity for inspiration. Into Jesus — wholly open to it — the Spirit came with all its fullness and power. Put into it whatever meaning you will, only do not limit its reality and its intensity. Call it God if you will; why hesitate when the immanence of God is declared to be universal, and the task of thought is not to bring God into humanity, but to show how He can be kept out of it. Rise in your conceptions Godward, and do not descend earthward; keep, at least, on the level of modern thought, and do not drop back into an age which seated God in the heavens with no sign of his presence on earth save sovereign power. It is enough, and it is more than we can compass, to say that Jesus, "being full of the Holy Ghost," was led by the Spirit into the wilderness. He had always been under the leading of the Spirit. It had infolded his life in its beginning, and followed him all the way until at last He took fire under contact with John, who brought the Hebraic spirit once more into the field of the nation's life. Under his baptism, Jesus rose into the ecstasy of full possession by the Spirit, and became, not a rapt prophet who saw visions and cried aloud, but a being full of power. This is the key to Jesus in the Temptation,—a sense of power. Spirit is not powerful; it is power itself. Without measure the Spirit had entered into him, and without measure had come a sense of power. He but perfectly illustrated a universal law. When a man is visited by the Spirit of God, it matters not to what end nor how it comes about, but when the reality of the gift is felt, whether it be to sing, or to build, or to paint, or to speak, or to urge reforms, he has a sense of power; it is the function of the Spirit to create power. It is through the Spirit that the energy which lies outside of matter and of man finds its way into them until the rose blooms, and the man rises up and says, I can do this thing that lies before me.

We are to regard Jesus at this juncture, not as a mild and placid man gently led by the Spirit into the wilderness, where He sits down to await his temptation. Rather are we to picture him as in the very excess of tumultuous feeling, his whole nature tossing with conflicting emotions, restless, eager : not beset by doubts, but rather overwhelmed by certainties ; not confused by this immense access of power, but only eager to use it aright. Limitless inflowing of the Spirit meant unlimited outgo of power. How to use it was the question that drove him into the wilderness. He had no doubt as to the main point, — namely, that He was called to set up the Kingdom of God on earth; and that it was to be done through the divine Fatherhood and the human Sonship. But what are to be the intermediate steps ? What shall He do with himself, — how fit himself to be the vehicle of this power to the world ? Power does not direct itself; or, if undirected, it runs to waste or to chance ends. The lesson of lessons for all men to learn is, how to use their powers ; and if they are great, the temptation to misuse them is correspondingly great. Christ did not deceive himself at this point. It was not so great a thing to have the power as to use it aright. He knew intuitively, — and also as one of a nation which had no philosophy but did have a theory of personal righteousness and a profound sense of reality, — that it was through a life that the Kingdom of God was to be set up. It is to be a direct, first-hand matter, — a life lived among men in immediate, out-and-out relations to the living God, — not a dialectic spun in the groves of the Academy, nor a dream woven out of the evanescent play of nature. Hence the supreme question was, how to get himself into right relations to this vast indwelling power.

The picture of Jesus lies upon the sacred page in so sweet and gentle a light; He was so patient, so unresisting, so helpless, almost courting weakness, — it is all so lamb-like in its passivity that we might pronounce him weak if we were not withheld by reverence. But such a thought would be far below the mark. Was Christ weak? Let the centuries answer. Were his principles weak? What is civilization striving after but their realization? He was not only not weak, but He never was unconscious of his power. His part in the temptation was, not to lay down a definite line of external operations, but to fortify himself in these principles so that He could turn his human life into the divine life, or — if one prefers it — to turn his divine life into human life; they are the two sides of one process. If He can do that, He has saved the world; for that is the salvation of the world and of every man born into it. The power of which He is conscious is to be transmuted into life, and the life is to be the light of men.

We have no occasion at this time to disentangle the story from its Oriental setting. Our Western minds are too severe and prosaic for such a task; but we can go so far as to set aside its objective features, and treat as real only those which are subjective.

Jesus was in the wilderness. He went there to be alone, and there He stayed until He had brought his sense of power, his will and his principles, into harmony, — a coördination that is set before every man. He did not go into the desert to fast, but, being there for another purpose, He fasted, forgetful of food while his great struggle was upon him. It was a solitary experience. No voice spoke to him; no tempter darkened the air; He climbed no mountain or pinnacle of the temple; no angels parted the heavens and came to him. These things were the projections of his inward experience; idealisms so real that only real things could express them; a drama conceived as such because it was the truest language.

Let us try to get at the kernel of this experience. We must keep in mind that Jesus was filled with an unlimited sense of power, that He had a full and clear sense of Sonship in God, and a profound conviction that He was called to declare the Kingdom of God upon earth.

Three universal temptations are encountered and overcome. He will not use his power in his own behalf; He will not change stones into bread even to save the life upon which the kingdom seems to hang; it would limit the scope of God's methods, and leave out the ethical in both God and man. To employ his power for himself would be to undo his Sonship, and that would undo the Kingdom, for He was to found it by himself becoming it; that is, religion is personal, and it cannot be anything else; it is a life, — a natural and not a miraculous life. Jesus cannot introduce into his own life anything that is not to enter into the life of every man. Hence no man can do anything for the Kingdom of God that is not done through and in himself; thus only can it have reality, and he himself become a sharer in it. To use a miracle would be to turn his back upon those other forces and phases of the divine Being of which He had become so conscious, and reduce the manifold "words," by which man lives, down to this one word of miracle. For, if man once tastes bread made from stones, and desire is satisfied in that easy way, he will not care for, nor will he see, any other. But the miracle always fascinates, and desire is always strong. Why not be healed by a word rather than keep the laws of health, or suffer the wholesome penalty of broken law? His decision turned upon several things, — first, a will of absolute temper, an abiding sense of Sonship in God, and trust in the unlimited resources of God. The heart of the matter lay in obedience, — his will brought into accord with the will of the Father. The experience was sane to the last degree. There were no omitted factors or possibilities. He made the decision on which personality at last turns, and ever turns. He abides what He is, — the obedient, trusting Son of the Father. Notice that this play of will is chiefly self-restraint, — the highest form of its discipline and action, especially when there is a sense of power.

This comes out also in the other temptations. As his dream sways to and fro, He imagines himself on some pinnacle of the temple; how easy it would be to drop unharmed into the midst of the people and win their homage. But here is another thing that He will not do : He will not trifle with the laws, for He has already watched the Father working perpetually, not by miracle, but by the orderly course of nature, and He will work in the same way. He will not forget that He is under the limitations of humanity, and that the kingdom must be founded under the conditions of humanity. Notice again how profoundly sane He is; and yet how great is the temptation, full of all sorts of beguilement, — the old way, the easy way of winning.

More subtle is the last temptation. Universal dominion; Rome gone and Judea in her place, — what a trophy to lay at the feet of the Father! But will the Father accept it? Has the Spirit breathed such a suggestion into his mind? The Kingdom is to be universal; how is it about the means? Will not the result partake of the character of the methods? Brute power, alliance with evil, — these are conquering forces, but they contradict the Spirit with which He is filled, and all that He knows of Fatherhood, and feels of Sonship. Jesus, in his decision, planted his foot on the primal, age-long lie that has corrupted nations, and deceived even the elect, that the end justifies the means. No man believes it, but the temptation to use it is so great that few men can resist it. Hence no temptation so deeply involves the will. As Christ's eye swept the world-wide conquest possible by alliance with evil, and then turned to the picture of himself returning to Nazareth as He came, sure to be despised and rejected of men, what tension of will was needed to keep him steady under the contrasting pictures. But it was more than will: it was will reinforced by a living sense of righteousness. The ideal purpose of his nation came like a delivering angel and carried him away into the company of the prophets whom the fathers had slain; and below all lay that ineradicable, unconquerable sense of obedience to God which had grown and blossomed into a consciousness that He was the very Son of the Father. About it clustered a group of kindred virtues — humility, meekness, patience, simplicity, truthfulness — that had been growing all his days, and now brought to him their strength and their inspiration. These were the angels that came to him, for there are no angels so strong and tender in their ministrations as inwrought virtues.

I have spoken of the temptation of Jesus as the conflict of one filled with a sense of power to do a certain work, and contemplating opposite methods of carrying it out. Everything is on the highest scale; the temptations are those that always beset humanity; the Kingdom is to be universal; the actors are God and a man filled with the Spirit of God. It can be set in many lights and will bear endless thought. It is to be classed with those dramas that deal with the fundamental experiences of mankind, as Hamlet and The Scarlet Letter, but with how different a result! It was an experience in which Jesus made those generic and universal choices that underlie manhood, and form character, and determine destiny. They represent the conflict of humanity with itself and against the evil that ever assails it, — conflicts through which it realizes itself and comes to a knowledge of itself as divine. And because they set forth the conflicts of humanity and its victories, they do the same for every man. There is but one way of life for all and each; one choice which the whole world is struggling to make in age-long conflicts and innumerable stages of history, — the same choice for every son of man, making which he finds that he is a son of God. These choices turned on the will and its ethical reinforcements. Jesus subjected his will to his moral conceptions; He ethicized it, made it complex by union with the virtues, and sublimated it by opening it to the Spirit of God. When He emerged from the temptation, He offered a sight which the world has looked on but has not yet fully realized, — a man making choice of God, but making it at the cost of all. He thus touched eternal law:

he that loseth his life shall save it. He thus rose out of natural manhood and entered into that state which is the final stage of humanity, — the divine returning by the path of life whence it came. By thus fulfilling humanity, He reveals its divinity and essential oneness with God. In this trilogy of temptation He lives out the process, — self and the world are laid down in sacrifice, and the order of God is taken up. He goes back to Nazareth a meek and patient doer of the will of the Father as it awaits him in the streets of the city. It is the moral idea turned into the stern reality of life itself. Where else shall we look for it? The Prometheus fulfilled one part of it, but left out obedience to the far-reaching counsels of Zeus, and so missed the eternal secret; he gave men fire, but he did not reveal God. The ideal could not be brought out by a people who lived on easy and equal terms with gods that were hardly gods but simply projections of themselves, as a mirage may set the play of earth in the sky.

Before turning away from this picture of the Christ let us linger until the Sabbath has come, and hear him repeat the ancient words which are now the rule of his life: " The Spirit of the Lord is upon me, because He hath anointed me to preach the Gospel to the poor; He hath sent me to heal the brokenhearted, to preach deliverance to the captives and recovering of sight to the blind, to set at liberty them that are bruised, to preach the acceptable year of the Lord." This was the outcome of his temptation, — the ability to say these words and to turn them into life. This ability was gained by immense and supreme acts of the will. He was filled with inspiration, but the experience as a temptation turned on his will and measured it. It consisted first in renunciation, but not in that alone. The renunciation was only to clear himself from entanglements and get into his field of action. What waste of energy and of life itself has come from dividing this experience, and using only the renunciating side of it! Self-denial is always preparatory to something positive. On nothing did Bishop Brooks speak more clearly than on the worthlessness of asceticism. It is the ignorant and corrupt perversion of self-denial. A will so nurtured will be one-sided, uncertain, morbid, and self-destructive.

Jesus did not pause an instant after He had made his great decisions, but entered at once into the world of positive achievement where the will that had been forged in the desert found ample room to test its strength. The point of interest for us is, that it was an ethicized will. It was a will that took spiritual and moral truths, social duties, personal righteousness, and laid them down upon life as realities. The reason we put emphasis upon the will is, that Jesus taught these realities by living them; that is, by acts of the will. He thus ingrafted them into the life of the world, creating Christianity by himself becoming it, redeeming the world by becoming a Redeemer. It is the distinction of Christianity, that it is not a religion among religions, but the one religion of humanity, because it redeems it by an actual life, — the only possible way to redeem.

There would be little need of saying all this if it were not that just such a will lies at the basis of manhood and constitutes it. Its fundamental requisite is not ethics nor will, but the two fused into one. The conception of rulers and of ruling forces is still imperfect. It is made up chiefly of will as determination, mere bulk of energy that gains its end as a strong man bursts open a locked door. But this is not the will that rules best. The will is, indeed, the basis of all effective action, but it is not bare power driving towards a goal. We may more and more — especially at the University — discount the man of mere will, whether it be in taking honors or winning the games, if he counts the victories as pledges of future success. In the greater world to which he goes, victories and honors must be undertaken on another basis. Society is growing intelligent, and upon the whole, moral, and it will be governed only on these terms. To-morrow — a long day off it may be — will confess that the goal of society is morality. Men are slowly finding it out. We cannot to-day countenance the war with Spain except as we look at it in a moral light. The unrest of society, whatever its form, springs from this discovery, — in wild ways, blind and furious when the ruling power is unjust, venting itself in poor cries for equality, the last thing it needs, not knowing what is the trouble nor what it wants; but in it all there is a sub-consciousness that it should be governed by intelligence and morality. It is correlated to these two things, and it will never rest until they are enthroned over it and in it.

But the world is still in its social childhood, and even in the University we have but touched the borders of the great secret. Our athletic friends are sure that resolute will is the chief requisite, and train themselves to that end. They see one side of a many-sided truth; may God guide them, and guard them, and restrain them in their beautiful tuition; and may they learn that victory and defeat serve the will in a proportion not easily to be determined! I think just here of your own Newell,[1] who, however the game might be going, played fair while he played strong, — proving his manhood by each, — and between games kept his life sweet by close and reverent contact with nature, and by prayer that "his spirit might also be pure and clear." May none of us, especially those who are of the University, drop back into the first rude conception of society that the strongest are to rule. Old ways of thinking are apt to recur with a revival of interest in our physical nature, and

---

[1] Marshall P. Newell, a graduate of '95, who recently died by accident in Springfield.

we are tempted to say that the strong body and the stout will hold the key of life.

The part of the University in this training of the will is clear. It is one of its chief functions to teach a man that he has a will, — or rather is a will, — not a blind and selfish obstinacy often called a will, but that clear sense of personality which justifies one in the use of the word "I," a word that is always to be felt as standing for a substantial reality. In ways that I need not name, the University defines and brings out this sense of personality. The first class in College is gregarious almost beyond the point of personal responsibility; in the last class, each man has come to a full sense of it. There is no more moving sight, to a thoughtful mind, than the graduation of half a thousand men, each one a trained personality, drawn out of the mass and made to feel that he is a force and has a right to regard himself as such. The only question is how he shall use this force, — whether for himself or for humanity, whether his will has been trained not only to strength but also to morals, — an all-important question, for on it hangs the greater question, whether he is to move in the course of the eternal purpose of God, or in some circle of his own; with humanity, or in the ever-deepening solitude of self. To aid in the answer of that question I have turned your attention to him who so far compassed life and all its fundamental questions and factors that He has become its unimpeachable law and the measure of its reality and power.

To what extent our Universities help to ethicize the will beyond strengthening it is not easy to determine. That they do much, there is no doubt; all education points to morality; but the morality I have in mind is something more than good habits and correct principles. I mean a morality that takes charge of the whole man, and makes his will its servant to do its work. I am not here to criticise them on this point, but I cannot forbear saying that any University or College that fails to infuse the ethical spirit and purpose into education on the ground that it consists in culture fails to understand either man or the world. Culture is the correlate of neither. John Henry Newman said that "university training is the great ordinary means to a great but ordinary end." What could so well describe the function of the university? The "ordinary end" can be no other than the moral well-being of society as a whole. It is ethics in the high sense that we plead for as a factor in education. Stouthearted pluck is a fine thing, but there is a finer. The great battles of humanity are not won by pluck. There is a truer manhood than that which passes under this name. A will grounded on morals, struck through with humanity, obedient to God, — a will informed with duty drawn from the eternal order of God even till the man becomes conscious that he is a son of God, — it is such a will that the University should train, because it is what society requires. The need is immense, especially in our public life where affairs often seem to be passing into the hands of bad men. As a consequence, the success which the University man craves is hard to win except by some degree of compromise and subjection. Hence the duty of training the will up to these higher standards, — not merely that he may resist temptation, but that he shall feel driven to take the initiative against these enemies of the nation and of social order. The criticism to be made on many graduates who go to the larger cities is, that they join the rings instead of fighting them. They betray not only their manhood but the University. It seems to them more necessary to win verdicts by being within the party than to lose verdicts and save manhood by staying without. God pity them in their strait, and teach them that such verdicts and such victories are not only failures but are black with shame.

The chief necessity in our American world to-day is, that the Universities should take the lead in public affairs. In one way and another they should fix the standards and secure the results of political action, and so redeem the nation from its shame. Let the University teach its students, by the thousand resources their education has made possible, to throw their will and conviction into the multiform battle against civic corruption and the rule of bad men. Education means — if it means anything — the multiplication of powers; and if the University leads thought, it should also lead action. The temptation of the educated man is to over-indulgence in thought. Hence he must train himself to action, and teach himself that life has no fulfillment except in action.

We have long enough waited on the maxim that occasions call out powers. It is but a half truth. It is powers that make occasions. The trained will creates a field for action wherever it is. Put conscience behind it, and the field is defined. Add a trained sense of humanity, and you have a man who cannot be held back from attacking any evil thing, nor from doing any good thing within his horizon.

This is the need to-day in public life, — not any vivid picturing of the evils; we know them well enough. The need is of hardened and tempered wills that can die but will not yield; wills so inwoven with conscience and so tender with humanity that the man is restless unless he is putting himself against the evil he sees and with the good he craves.

It is a splendid thing, — this central faculty trained to its full, buttressed by intelligence, inspired by those angel-qualities that are feet and wings to its purpose, — conscience, love, humility, — ready for any task that humanity lays before it; a will that can stand and stay with majority or minority, it matters not which if it is on the side of right, but standing and never yielding. This is the victory that overcomes the world and saves the world, — that makes the man and saves the man.

# IV
## THE MESSAGE OF CHRIST TO THE SCHOLAR

By the Rev. WILLIAM DeWITT HYDE, D.D.

# THE MESSAGE OF CHRIST TO THE SCHOLAR

Let us first give thanks for our theme. A generation ago it would have been the relation of science to religion, — abstraction to abstraction. To-day it is the message of Christ to the Scholar, — man to man. The warfare of science with theology is accomplished, and in two erudite volumes its sorry story has been told. Never again, in seats of liberal learning at least, shall we deny the right of science to test all truth by the impartial witness of the facts; never again doubt the duty of religion to cherish the highest ideal which prophet and psalmist have portrayed, and apostle and evangelist have handed down. The way at last is clear for the scholar's message to the Christian on all questions of historical and literary criticism, geological and biological development, without imputation of infringement on ecclesiastical prerogatives; and also for Christ's message to the scholar on all points of moral obligation and spiritual life, without suspicion of encroachment on the scholar's legitimate domain. For no enlightened Christian wishes to shield from the keen edge of criticism the formulas of his faith; and no worthy scholar aims at less than the highest as the motive of his work.

Before we can declare Christ's message to the scholar, we must see who Christ is, and what He stands for; who the scholar is, and what he represents. These terms once clearly grasped, the message of the one to the other will not be far to seek.

Who, then, is the scholar? No formal definition will avail. If we begin with what the scholar is not, and approach by gradual stages, we may thus come to understand him.

At the farthest remove from the scholar stands the idiot. He has a train of ideas which is ἴδιος, literally his own private, peculiar property. He does not share the common stock of ideas current among his fellows. Consequently he is impervious to truth and incapable of error. He is outside the sphere in which truth and error dwell; amenable to no standard; subject to no criticism. Now what the idiot lacks, the scholar must have.

The scholar must think the thought that is common to all minds, the universal thought. This, however, does not come all at once. There are three distinct stages of approach to this universal thought; three grades of educated intelligence, — the technical student; the student of liberal arts; and the scholar.

The technical student recognizes and reckons with those universal principles and laws which bind things and events together in a system of accepted science. In his practical adjustment to them he is exceeding shrewd and sagacious, — far shrewder often than the scholar, whose acquaintance with them is more intimate. Yet, in all his dealing with these scientific principles, the technical student is using rather than serving them; regarding what they are to him and his purposes, rather than what they are in and of themselves. Now truth is a jealous mistress; and though, under constraint, she may give the technical student her hand, she never lets him have her heart. Though he may gain an amount of knowledge far beyond what the student of liberal arts acquires, still, in so far as he confines himself strictly to the technical applications of his art, and regards his knowledge as instrumental to that end, while we esteem him in all other respects as a most useful and honorable member of society, in the scale of scholarship which we are considering here we can give him only the lowest place. The faculties of liberal arts refuse to recognize for their degrees any form of learning that has this stamp of practicality upon it. Liberal learning must be purely disinterested, seeking learning for her own sweet sake, unmindful of the dowry of utility that may be settled on her. The attitude of the technical student, on the contrary, is that which Browning ascribes to Berthold in " Colombe's Birthday." Berthold's heart is on the duchy, rather than the duchess; and to her question, " You love me, then ? " he replies: —

> "Your lineage I revere,
> Honor your virtue, in your truth believe,
> Do homage to your intellect, and bow
> Before your peerless beauty."

And when the duchess presses her question, " But, for love " — he answers bluntly: —

> " A further love I do not understand."

And when the duchess asks Valence, the true lover, why all this which Berthold offers is not love, he answers : —

"Because not one of Berthold's words and looks
Had gone with love's presentment of a flower
To the beloved; because bold confidence,
Open superiority, free pride,—
Love owns not, yet were all that Berthold owned."

It is this regard for the advantages and utilities of learning, this "open superiority and free pride" toward learning in and for itself, which marks off all technical approaches to learning into a category apart from that devotion to learning for learning's sake which is the distinctive mark of liberal study and pure scholarship.

The student of liberal arts, in form and intent at least, seeks learning, not for what she can give him in immediate utility, but because only by the enlargement and emancipation of his mind through learning can he gain his eternal heritage of truth and joy. He seeks, not what learning can give him, but what she is in herself, and can inspire him to become. He addresses her as, in Stephen Phillips's poem, Idas vows his devotion to Marpessa: —

"I love thee, then,
Not only for thy body packed with sweet
Of all this world, that cup of brimming June,
Nor for that face which might indeed provoke
Invasion of old cities; no, nor all

> Thy freshness stealing on me like strange sleep.
> Not for this only do I love thee, but
> Because Infinity upon thee broods;
> And thou art full of whispers and of shadows.
> Thou meanest what the sea has striven to say
> So long, and yearned up the cliffs to tell;
> Thou art what all the winds have uttered not,
> What the still night suggesteth to the heart.
> Thy voice is like to music heard ere birth,
> Some spirit lute touched on a spirit sea.
> Thy face remembered is from other worlds;
> It has been died for, though I know not when;
> It has been sung of, though I know not where.
> It has the strangeness of the luring West,
> And of sad sea-horizons; beside thee
> I am aware of other times and lands,
> Of birth far back, of lives in many stars."

Still, even this is but the passionate courtship, not the consummated marriage, of the mind with truth. The student never sees his beloved alone. He gets truth at second hand, from the lips of a teacher or the pages of a book. Good teaching, to be sure, reduces this dependence on authority to a minimum. A great step is the substitution of many books in the library for one in the hand of the student. Another is the substitution of the thesis, embracing many aspects of a subject in a single view, for the recitation of detached bits of information from day to day. Yet all these theses and abstracts and seminary methods are but the preliminaries of scholarship, not the actual race; like the first steps of the infant, a wonder to him and a delight to his fond parents, but not to be counted on for covering much ground.

The scholar lives in intimate and conscious presence of a thought larger, higher, holier than his own. Not what he happens to think, like the idiot; not what he finds it useful to assume, like the technical student; not what the books and the teachers say, like the student of liberal arts, — but what firsthand observation of the facts, what fresh investigation of the sources, what vivid reproduction of the process reveals directly to him, — that, and that alone, the scholar reverently and fearlessly proclaims. He is the voice of the thought that is silently thinking in things; he is the witness of the truth that is shyly secreted in facts; he is the historian of that which hath been when things now dead were alive, and the prophet of that which shall be when forces now latent in germs shall burst into blossom and fruit. Fichte, in his lectures on "The Nature of the Scholar," has given eloquent expression to this dependence of the scholar on a thought higher than his own : " The true scholar has no other purpose in action but to express his idea, and embody the truth he recognizes in word and work. No personal regard, either for himself or others, can impel him to do that which is not demanded by this purpose; no such regard can cause him to neglect anything which is required by this purpose. His person, and all personality in the world, have long since vanished from before him, and entirely disappeared in his effort after the realization of the Idea. The idea *alone* impels him; where it does not move him, he rests and remains inactive. Until the Idea stands before him, finished and perfect even to word and deed, nothing moves him to action; the Idea rules him entirely, governs all his powers, and exhausts all his life and effort. To its manifestation he devotes his whole personal being without reserve or intermission, for he looks upon his life as only the instrument of the Idea." This self-forgetfulness of the scholar was happily expressed by Professor Sylvester when, after an intricate original mathematical demonstration, a friend asked him, " Do you not wonder at the powers of your own mind ? " he replied,

"No, but I wonder that these things are so." Here, as in the other cases, however, for the most adequate modern expression of the scholar's attitude we must look to the poets. Kipling has caught the spirit of it in his lines "To the True Romance:" —

> "Thy face is far from this our war,
>   Our call and counter-cry;
> I shall not find Thee quick and kind,
>   Nor know Thee till I die:
> Enough for me in dreams to see
>   And touch Thy garment's hem;
> Thy feet have trod so near to God
>   I may not follow them.
>
> "Through wantonness if men profess
>   They weary of Thy parts,
> E'en let them die at blasphemy
>   And perish with their arts;
> But we that love, but we that prove
>   Thine excellence august,
> While we adore discover more
>   Thee perfect, wise, and just.
>
> "Since spoken word man's spirit stirred
>   Beyond his belly-need,
> What is, is Thine of fair design
>   In thought and craft and deed;
> Each stroke aright of toil and fight,
>   That was and that shall be,
> And hope too high, wherefore we die,
>   Has birth and worth in Thee."

This impersonal devotion to a truth so

high above him that he bows before it in self-forgetful reverence, and at the same time is so high above other men that he who sees it is supremely indifferent to the praise and blame of those who see it not; this union of the lowliest humility toward truth with the loftiest assurance toward all who would gainsay it, — this is ever the twofold mark of the scholar.

What, then, has Christ to say to this meek and haughty man? If I could take the Fourth Gospel I could easily show, trait for trait, that Christ is precisely what we have discovered the scholar to be. That work, however, has already been admirably done, — first by Fichte in his "Way Towards the Blessed Life," and again in our own day by Phillips Brooks in his lecture, "The Influence of Jesus on the Intellectual Life of Man." Furthermore many scholars doubt whether the Gospel according to John is the message of the Nazarene Jesus to the scholar, or rather the combined message of Jewish Christianity and Greek scholarship to the world. The existence of this doubt, together with the fact that for those who do not share the doubt the work has already been done far better than I could do it, indicates as our task to-night the discovery of Christ's message in the older and surer tradition. Accordingly I shall draw all my material for this message from that swift series of scenes, with only such sayings and discourses as are necessary to hold the concrete facts together, which has come down to us in the form of the Gospel of Mark.

Who, then, is Christ? Even less than in the case of the scholar is verbal definition adequate. As before, we must begin far off, and by gradual stages approach the height of this unique and lofty character.

The knave stands farthest from Christ: for the knave follows his own wayward, selfish will, regardless of the rights, heedless of the interests, of others. "Not what I will," on the contrary, was the purpose and prayer of Christ. The knave stands related to Christ, as the fool to the scholar. "What I happen to think," says the fool. "What I chance to want," says the knave. "Not what I happen to think," says the scholar. "Not what I chance to wish," says Christ. There is a difference. One moves primarily in the sphere of thought, the other in the sphere of will. Yet the "Not what I," the negation of the merely private and personal, is common to them both. And Christ's message to the knave is much the same as the scholar's word to the fool. The scholar says to the fool: "Get out of this petty self-centred habit of thinking whatever happens to strike you. Let the winds of criticism blow through the close, contracted apartments of your mind. Throw up your windows, and let the universal reason in." Christ's word to the knave we have in the first chapter of Mark: "Now after John was delivered up, Jesus came into Galilee, preaching the Gospel of God, and saying, The time is fulfilled, and the Kingdom of God is at hand: repent." Get out of your mean, miserable selves, that is, and let the great and glorious will of God, the wide and generous interests of your fellows, come in and fill you with the universal love. It is a reëcho, with profounder ethical significance, of the cry of the psalmist: "Lift up your heads, O ye gates; and be ye lift up, ye everlasting doors; and the King of glory shall come in."

Next above the downright knave comes the worldly man. His attitude toward the moral law corresponds to that of the technical student toward scientific truth. He knows the moral order, but, instead of serving it, uses it for his own selfish ends. The worldly man is off the same piece as the knave, but he is more crafty and shrewd. His deeds are better, but his heart is worse. He observes the moral law toward those whom he considers his equals; that is, toward those who are strong enough to strike back if he dares to do them harm. But for the moral law in itself, or for other persons as such, the worldly man does not care a straw. To serve the law, or to serve his fellows for their own sakes, is a degree of simplicity which he cannot comprehend. He knows how to use it and them for his own purposes, and that is enough for him. The worldly man is the knave, plus the wit to appear respectable, and minus the courage to show himself as bad as he is. He is outwardly polished, inwardly corrupt. If you want a picture of his soul, you will find it in Watts's "Mammon," — his heavy foot on the prostrate form of the youth his cruel avarice has crushed; one coarse hand on the bowed head of the maiden his loathsome lust has ruined, the other clutching the money-bags which give him power to do these dastardly deeds unpunished by law and unbanished from society. Our rapid material development is making this a very common type. It engages in all branches of business, practices law, figures in politics, frequents the university, throngs the club.

Such is the worldly man. What says Christ to him? In the Jerusalem of Jesus' day, these specious pretenders to an undeserved respectability, these manipulators of moral and social conventions for private profit and personal advantage, were represented by the unscrupulous scribes. "And He said unto them in His doctrine, Beware of the scribes, which love to go in long clothing, and love salutations in the market-places, and the chief seats in the synagogues, and the uppermost rooms at feasts; which devour widows' houses, and for a pretense make long prayers: these shall receive greater damnation." Yes, greater damnation than the outspoken knave shall the worldly man of today receive; for to the knave's baseness of heart the worldly man adds the cowardice, hypocrisy, and insincerity of cloaking his stealing under forms of law, and paying fancy prices with the proceeds for the concealment of his vices under the gilding of respectability.

Here surely is a point where the scholar can appreciate the Christ. The scholar refuses to recognize for his degrees the pursuit of learning in the spirit of mere utility. Shall he not, then, revere the Christ who refused to put the conditions of admission to His Kingdom of righteousness low enough to admit any man who is capable of using the moral law and the rights of his fellows as means to his selfish ends?

Next above the worldly stands the moral man. By the moral man I mean the man who follows the customs, usages, traditions, and standards of conduct which he finds ready-made. He corresponds to the student of liberal arts in the intellectual scale. As the student takes his knowledge at second hand from books and teachers, so the moral man is a dealer in second-hand virtue. This is not altogether a reproach. Virtue of any sort, first hand or second hand, is good so far as it goes. Mere conventional morality is good so long as it does not compete with something better, or pose as the best. Nevertheless, just as no amount of second-hand information, with which a student may cram his cranium, can entitle him to the degree and rank of the scholar; so no amount of conformity to moral custom, or cultivation of conventional virtue, can admit the mere moralist to the highest plane of spiritual life.

These apostles of second-hand virtue are very numerous to-day. You find them in the university; on the faculty, as well as among the students. They are generally the children of parents who got their virtue first hand at the sources: otherwise they would not have the moral momentum requisite to do their intellectual work in the thorough and honest way it is done. For the children of ancestors who had originality in righteousness, or in other words were religious people, can run for a generation or two on inherited moral momentum, without showing outward signs of serious moral deterioration. Yet, while they can keep themselves going, they have little or no moral inspiration to impart to others. They are blind to the finer moral issues when they present themselves in new and unconventional forms. They incline to the wrong side of the great spiritual issues which confront and judge the men of each new age. They can keep in old ruts; they cannot plough new furrows. They can respect the past; they cannot mould the future. They mean well; are, as a rule, irreproachable in outward conduct. But they are spiritually sluggish and obtuse. They are conventionalized forms of the soul, rather than actual souls. Their good deeds resemble the fruit you may find still clinging to the branches of a tree that has been cut down. It is real fruit, no mistake; but it is a bit shriveled and insipid. And you feel that when this is gone there will be no fresh fruit borne on these rootless, lifeless branches. Deterioration, decadence, degeneration, has silently but unmistakably set in.

Such is the moral man. What is Christ's message to him? The great representatives of a merely traditional and conventional morality in his day were the Pharisees. They, to be sure, had other traits which our modern moral man has not,—insincerity, sanctimoniousness, a desire to pass for better men than they were. Yet the fundamental trait of taking duty and virtue at second hand from the traditions and standards of society, rather than at first hand from the sources of spiritual inspiration and life, is common to the Pharisee of the times of Jesus and the moral man of to-day.

Now we all know what Jesus thought of the Pharisee. The one recorded case of His sighing deeply, as if in complete despair of getting on with utterly impossible people, was when these stupid slaves of convention and tradition, incapable of seeing the intrinsic beauty of spiritual truth and life, asked Him to authenticate it by a sign from heaven. "And He sighed deeply in His spirit, and saith, Why doth this generation seek a sign? Verily I say unto you, There shall no sign be given unto this generation." They must take the spiritual life at first hand, on its intrinsic merits, or not at all. His refusal to accept tradition as ultimate was the chief charge they had against Him. "And the Pharisees and the scribes ask Him, Why walk not thy disciples according to the tradition of the elders, but eat their bread with defiled hands? And He said unto them, Well did Isaiah prophesy of you hypocrites, as it is written,—

"This people honoreth me with their lips,
But their heart is far from me.
But in vain do they worship me,
Teaching as their doctrines the precepts of men.
Ye leave the commandment of God, and hold fast the tradition of men."

These same Pharisees are the witnesses to the magnificent originality and impersonality of Jesus' teaching. "And when they were come, they say unto Him, Master, we know that thou art true, and carest not for any one: for thou regardest not the person of men, but of a truth teachest the way of God."

Here, again, is a point of sympathy between Christ and the scholar. The scholar refuses to stop with second-hand learning, held on the authority of book or teacher. Christ refuses to be content with second-hand virtue, resting on the tradition of men or a sign from heaven. Christ goes to the sources of spiritual life, as the scholar to the sources of knowledge.

What, then, is the source of spiritual life? That is the final form of our question, Who is Christ? Wherein does He differ from the knave, the worldly man, and the moral man? The characteristic mark of Christ is love for men. Not what He would like, regardless of law; not what He can get by manipulation of law; not what He must do to keep the law: but that good of man at which all just law aims, — that is the motive of Christ. He will break law for the good of others; never, like the knave, merely to gratify himself. He will modify law for the expanding interest of man; never, like the scribe, for private gain. He will keep law to the last jot or tittle, in so far as it stands for the rights of his fellows and the preservation of society; never, like the Pharisee, to fatten his own spiritual pride. Christ is thus at once the destroyer of old laws as soon as they have lost their living meaning; the inspirer of new laws, as soon as new forms of human good demand them. This love of Christ was no weak sentimentalism that shrinks either from inflicting or from bearing pain. The friend of man, He was the foe of all that sought to do man harm. That was why He could deal hard blows without malice, and take hard blows in turn without resentment. Christ is original, free, first hand, because the word He speaks and the deed He does springs fresh and straight from a heart so large and strong and pure that it can make the good of every man He touches as dear to Him as His own. In other words, He lives in the Father's love for all His human children.

Read in the light of this insight, all His words about Himself, and all the words of His friends about Him, become clear. "And as He was going forth into the way, there ran one to Him and kneeled to Him and asked Him, Good Master, what shall I do that I may inherit eternal life? And Jesus said unto him, Why callest thou me good? None is good save one, even God." In other words, all goodness is participation in the great love which sees men and things as the Father sees and loves them. This was His ultimate answer to all who questioned Him concerning the sources of the spiritual life. "And one of the scribes came and heard them questioning together, and, knowing that He had answered them well, asked Him, What commandment is the first of all? Jesus answered, The first is, Hear, O Israel: The Lord our God, the Lord is one; and thou shalt love the Lord thy God with all thy heart, and with all thy soul, and with all thy mind, and with all thy strength. The second is this, Thou shalt love thy neighbor as thyself. There is none other commandment greater than these." To share the universal love, — this is the sum and substance of all legislation, this is the living source whence all law proceeds. Sympathy in this experience, participation in this loving will of God, was the one test of fellowship with Him. "And there come His mother and His brethren; and, standing without, they sent unto Him, calling Him. And a multitude was sitting about Him; and they say unto Him, Behold, thy mother and thy brethren without seek for thee. And He answereth them and saith, Who is my mother and my brethren? And, looking round on them which sat round about Him, He saith, Behold my mother and my brethren! For whosoever shall do the will of God, the same is my brother, and sister, and mother." This spirit of love was the explanation of all He did; and to confound that spirit with the spirit of evil was the one unpardonable sin. "Verily I say unto you, All their sins shall be forgiven unto the sons of men, and their blasphemies wherewith soever they shall blaspheme: but whosoever shall blaspheme against the Holy Spirit hath never forgiveness, but is guilty of an eternal sin; because they said, He hath an unclean spirit." In other words, the man who is capable of attributing an act done out of pure loving-kindness and holy pity to a base and evil motive is so lost to all sense of decency, and all appreciation of goodness, that there is no hope for him. That sin alone is eternal; that soul alone is lost.

Finally, in the great crisis of his life, that which made possible the first half of the prayer, "Not what I will," was that abiding sense of the all-embracing love of the Father which He expressed in the last half of the same prayer, "but what thou wilt." The scholar, faithful to the thought expressed in things, willing to renounce his own pet hypothesis the instant a fact is found to contradict it, surely must appreciate the same trait coming out here in the costlier sphere of will, which renounces the most fundamental of personal impulses, that of self-preservation, the moment it is seen to clash with the universal purposes of God. Christ is the witness to the universality of a loving Will for men, as the scholar is the witness to the universality of a system of thought in things.

Right here, however, we meet the peculiar difficulty of the scholar in this agnostic age. He admits that this devotion to unselfish and universal ends is sweet and beautiful. But he puts his scholar's question, "Is it true? Is there a universal Will? Is there an eternal Love?" His doubt, and His search for a sign to solve it, finds expressive echo in our latest version of agnostic hope by William Watson: —

> " Did Heaven vouchsafe some sign
> That through all Nature's frame
> Boundless ascent benign
> Is everywhere her aim,
> Such as man hopes it here,
> Where he from beasts hath risen, —
> Then might I read full clear,
> Ev'n in my sensual prison,
> That Life and Law and Love are one symphonious name."

Failing to find throughout the cosmic process unmistakable evidence of such an aim, he hastens to conclude that man is

> " Rather some random throw
> Of heedless Nature's die,
> Child of a thousand chances 'neath the indifferent sky;"

and finally takes refuge in the vagueness of pantheistic phrases: —

> " Unmeet to be profaned by praise
> Is He whose coils the world enfold;
> The God on whom I ever gaze,
> The God I never once behold,
> Above the cloud, beneath the clod;
> The Unknown God, the Unknown God."

This craving for a sensuous sign, this demand that the spiritual shall attest itself at a materialistic seance, is not new to the world. No sign was vouchsafed to the Pharisee who asked it of Jesus; no God was revealed to the astronomer who swept the heavens with his telescope in search of one. And if to-day geology has failed to dig one out of Devonian or Silurian strata, and biology has failed to evolve one from the struggle for existence, it does not therefore follow that the hope of the world is vain.

The fundamental fallacy of all agnostics, whether Pharisees and scribes or Kants and Spencers, whether eighteenth century astronomers or nineteenth century biologists, — the fundamental fallacy common to them all consists in first looking for the spiritual in that which by hypothesis is incapable of containing it, and then proclaiming, as the latest wonder, that they cannot find the spiritual there.

Mr. Watson is quite right when he defines the spiritual, the divine, as "Unconquerable Love." What, then, is love? and where could it be found? Is it not the assumption by one person of the being and interests of another?

And does not that imply self-consciousness, and a highly developed self-consciousness at that? Can this "Unconquerable Love" manifest itself in any other conceivable form? Is there any conceivable sign that could attest its presence in either cloud or clod? Have the lower animals sufficiently developed brains to be the bearers of this message? Could even primitive man have comprehended it, or made it intelligible to his primitive companions? The only conceivable form in which this message could come to the world is in a highly developed man. And in precisely that way — the only conceivable way — God has come into the world, the universal love has been made manifest. Foregleams of its coming flashed forth in unremembered soldier-saints and prophet-statesmen whose words are preserved to us under the names of David and Isaiah; in Socrates and Plato; in countless ancient seers and heroes. In the fullness of a personality conscious of its divine source in God, and assured of its ultimate triumph in the hearts of men, Love came to the world in Jesus Christ; Love is present in the world to-day in the spirit of Christ's true followers. In the only way that is conceivable or possible, — that is, through the Son and the Spirit, — God is manifest to men. To ignore this revelation in Son and Spirit, and cast about to find Him

> "Above the cloud, beneath the clod,"

or in

> "The gibbering form obscene,
> That was and was not man,"

is as absurd as it would be to cast your net for fish on dry land, or thrust in the sickle for grain upon the tossing surface of the sea. The fathers of Unitarianism did a brave, true act when they denied the doctrine of the Trinity as it then was held. For as it was then held almost universally, and as it continues to this day to be held in many strongholds of orthodoxy, it is a mere verbal contradiction, destitute of all vitality and power. To bury the dead is always a worthy service, but it is not quite the same thing as giving birth to the living. Denying a lie is not equivalent to affirming the truth. If the religious life is ever to recover from the blindness of agnosticism with which it is now stricken, if it is to escape the perpetual alternation between the empty affirmations of pantheistic poetry and the barren negations of positivistic prose, it must be through a rediscovery by all parties, conservative and liberal alike, of the fact that the only revelation of God that can meet the fair demands of honest modern doubt is that which hath been made in His Son Jesus Christ, and is present in our midst to-day in the life of the Christian Spirit.

The message of Christ to man is, that the universal love which is the life of God was manifested in Him, and is reproduced in those who share His Spirit. This message, as I have tried to show, stands out on the pages of the Gospel that confines itself most simply to the historic facts. Of course these facts ultimately require interpretation, and the only adequate interpretation is substantially that which we find in the Gospel of John. This doing of a Will higher than His own, this manifestation of the "Unconquerable Love," implies the previous existence of that Will; implies relations between that Love and Him who makes it manifest; implies, in other words, a whole theology of the Johannean type. Even in our simple story of Mark, however, the elements of such a theology are present.

The disciples as well as the Lord are the bearers of a message which is not their own, but the utterance of the Spirit which they have caught from Him, and ultimately received from God. "And when they lead you to judgment, and deliver you up, be not anxious beforehand what ye shall speak; but whatsoever shall be given you in that hour, that speak ye: for it is not ye that speak, but the Holy Spirit." In the finite and temporal crisis, their refuge and defense shall be the Infinite Right, the Eternal Love.

Such is Christ's message. It is the same to all; no different to the scholar than to other men. Yet there are points of similarity between Christ and the scholar which make His message especially intelligible to the scholar, and bring it home to him with peculiar force. For as in the sphere of thought the scholar merges the individual and the personal in a universal and impersonal Truth, so Christ in the sphere of will points all men to the Infinite Righteousness and the Eternal Love as the Source of all that is good in Himself, and the Spirit of all that is holy in them.

This message of Christ is ultimate. In no

other way could the "Unconquerable Love" reveal itself save in human fidelity and sacrifice; by no other way can man aspire to fellowship with God save by the plain path of obedience to the Son, reception of the Spirit, wherein the Father is revealed. For the filial life of fraternal love, which Christ first manifested in its fullness, and imparted to His followers as the Spirit of all true life forevermore, — this is the life of God in the only form in which the Divine is knowable, or credible, or practicable for us men. And this, in the sphere of spiritual life, is the perfect counterpart of that faithful devotion to the Absolute Truth which, in the sphere of thought, is the distinctive work of the scholar. For Christ and the scholar are witnesses in different ways to that unity of all men and all things in a rational and spiritual system, which, on the side of thought, finds expression in the kingdom of science under the law of reason, and on the side of will demands realization in a kingdom of righteousness under the rule of God.

# V

## THE MESSAGE OF CHRIST TO THE INNER LIFE

BY THE REV. HENRY VAN DYKE, D.D.

# THE MESSAGE OF CHRIST TO THE INNER LIFE

CHRIST's ultimate mission was to the inner life of man.

His message there was not in words alone, but in character and action, in what He was and in what He did for men: the heart of His message was Himself, His life, His death.

The central gospel of this message is the reality and certainty of the forgiveness of sins.

These three statements may serve to mark out, in a broad way, the line of thought that I wish to follow in this lecture.

Christ came into the world to proclaim and establish the kingdom of God. The sway of that kingdom extends over every region of our life. But its seat must be within us. It must reach and reconcile and rule that interior region of the heart which lies behind audible utterance and visible action, below social ties and bonds of human fellowship, underneath conscious reasonings and formulated theories, — that undiscovered country where the moral sentiments, the religious feeling, the sense of dependence, and the joy or grief of living, have their home.

There can be no real empire of divine peace unless this deepest region is reached. There must be no nook or corner or crevice of man's life left unexplored, unsubdued, unreconciled; no lurking-place of rebellion; no fountain of discord; no

"little rift within the lute,
That slowly widening makes the music mute."

The kingdom must go in to the centre and down to the bottom of personality, and work from within outward, — from below upward. This was the programme of Christ; and to carry it out He directed His journey to the inner life of man.

On the way thither, like a Prince in progress, He conferred inestimable gifts and blessings in the outer circles of human existence. The doctrine of Jesus has widened the thoughts of men. The example of Jesus has crystallized the moral aspirations of men into a flawless and imperishable ideal. The precept of Jesus has struck the keynote for a new harmony of human fellowship. The influence of Jesus has given inspiration and guidance to philosophy and literature and the fine arts.

But as we follow Him through these regions we are made aware that He is pressing onward to a goal beyond. He seeks the thinker, we say, behind the thought. He is looking for the person behind the social order. He aims to elevate man by uplifting men. His mission is not to masses, nor to classes; it is to the individual. But when He finds the individual, as a thinker, as a social unit, what then? Still Christ seems to press onward, to seek a yet deeper point.

His mission to society is through the individual. But when we have said that, we have not yet said all. His mission to the individual is through the inner life. He has not arrived at the goal of His journey. He has not spoken the last word of His message until He has said to the paralytic, "Son, be of good cheer, thy sins are forgiven thee;" and to the woman of Syro-Phœnicia, "Go in peace;" and to the disciples, "Let not your heart be troubled;" and to all the weary and heavy-laden, "Come unto me, and ye shall find rest unto your souls."

The kingdom of God which Jesus proclaims and establishes is a kingdom of the soul. Its deepest meaning is a personal experience. Its essence is righteousness and peace and joy in the Holy Ghost. Its dwelling-place and seat of power is in the inner life.

Now, if this be true, it is perfectly natural, and altogether reasonable, that the earliest and clearest and most enduring manifestation of Christ should be in this region of man's inmost, secret, inexplicable being. The impress of His character should be deepest upon the sub-liminal self. The traces of His presence in the world should be most distinct and most indelible in the records of spiritual experience. The evidences of His healing, purifying, harmonizing, saving power should be found first and most abundantly in those underlying relations, those mysterious sentiments and propensities, —

> "those obstinate questionings
> Of sense and outward things,
> Fallings from us, vanishings;
> Blank misgivings of a creature
> Moving about in worlds not realized,

High instincts before which our mortal Nature
Doth tremble like a guilty thing surprised:
   Those first affections,
   Those shadowy recollections,
Which, be they what they may,
Are yet the fountain light of all our day."

And so in fact we find it to be. The image of Jesus comes to light, first of all, in the spiritual experience of man. The earliest and the most wonderful picture of Him is simply a living reflection of Him in man's inner life. Before we can discern any influence of His teaching, as a great reformer, upon the institutions of society; before we can perceive, in the systematic records of the world's thought, any effect of those large, simple truths which He brought to light; before we can trace the rudest beginnings of Christian art, the most ancient formulas of Christian worship, the earliest foundations of Christian temples; yes, even before we can find any narrative of the life of Jesus, any collection of His sayings, any record of His deeds, — first of all, and most vivid of all, we see the person of Jesus revealed in the personal letters of certain men who loved and trusted and adored Him as their Lord and Saviour.

As a matter of fact, the Epistles come before the Gospels. We do not say they are any more authentic, any more precious, than the Gospels. We do not say they are ever to be read or interpreted apart from the Gospels. But we say they are forever sacred and authoritative to all Christian hearts, because they are the place where we first catch sight of Jesus Christ in this world. And their personal testimony, their peculiar significance, their religious meaning, must never be forgotten or denied, if we want to know what Christ came to do, and what Christ really did, for the life of man.

For what are these Epistles? They are not formal treatises of theology, of ethics, of church government. They are simply transcripts of the spiritual experience of real men, — Peter and Paul and John, and perhaps some others whose names we do not know.

No one can doubt that the centre of these letters is Jesus Christ. He is their theme and their inspiration, their impulse and their aim. They are written in His name. They bear witness to His power, they glow with His praise. They are first of all, and most of all, records of the message which Jesus brought to the inner life of these men, testimonies to the change which He wrought in their souls, — a change so great, so deep, so joyful that it was like a new birth, a veritable passing from death unto life. Listen to a description of this change, in words so fresh and glowing that it seems as if they might have been written but yesterday: —

"Therefore if any man be in Christ, he is a new creature: old things are passed away; behold, all things are become new. And all things are of God, who hath reconciled us to himself by Jesus Christ, and hath given to us the ministry of reconciliation; to wit, that God was in Christ, reconciling the world unto Himself, not imputing their trespasses unto them, and hath committed unto us the word of reconciliation. Now, then, we are ambassadors for Christ, as though God did beseech you by us: we pray you in Christ's stead, be ye reconciled to God. For He hath made Him to be sin for us, who knew no sin, that we might be made the righteousness of God in Him."

This is an authentic report of the message of Christ to the inner life of man. This is an echo of what He really spoke in the secret place of the human heart. This is the voice of that new tide of peace which silently rose through man's experience, —

> "One common wave of thought and joy
> Lifting mankind again."

This is the original gospel which began to win the world eighteen hundred years ago, and has never ceased to spread from heart to heart, from land to land, like music mixed with light.

And it is the faithful and persistent witness to this experience, more than anything else, that has made Christianity a world-religion. A changed heart, uttering its new-found felicity in sweet and searching tones, — this is the miracle that has drawn the attention of men, century after century, to the teachings of Christianity. Its apostles have won their way chiefly by the evidence which they gave that a message had come to them which transformed their lives at the fountain-head. The sense of newness in their souls was the source of their power. Whenever this sense of newness has faded and grown dim, the self-propagating force of Christianity has waned. Whenever this sense of newness has been deep and strong and vivid, Christianity has advanced swiftly and found wide and happy welcome. Its most potent argument has been this simple and direct testimony to the renewal and pacification of the inner life of man by the acceptance of Jesus Christ in the heart.

I am not concerned, at present, to justify it, to defend it, to argue for its truth or its morality, to find a place for it in a system of theology or philosophy. What I want to do is just to tell what it was; to show what it meant to the men who received it; to look at it, not as a theory, not as a doctrine, but as a spiritual experience; to let the inner life speak for itself about what Christ has done for the souls of those who have believed on Him.

That His message was one of joy and peace needs no proof. The New Testament is a book that throbs and glows with inexpressible gladness. It is the one bright spot in the literature of the first century. The Christians were the happiest people in the world. Poor, they were rich; persecuted, they were exultant; martyred, they were victorious. The secret of Jesus, as they knew it, was a blessed secret. It filled them with the joy of living. Their watchword was, "Rejoice and be exceeding glad."

But what were the elements of that joy? What was it that had entered into their inner life thus to transform and illuminate it?

To answer this question fully would be to give a summary of the primitive records of Christianity. All the manifold aspects of human existence were affected, unmistakably and immediately, by faith in Jesus Christ as the Son of God and the Saviour of men. Those who received Him thus into their hearts felt that they were saved. And if one had asked them from what they were saved, doubtless they would have wondered at the question, and would have answered, "From everything that brings trouble and fear and anguish and death into our souls."

The world looked to them like a new place, and they felt like new men. Sorrow was changed. Instead of a hopeless burden of affliction, it had become the means of working out for them a far more exceeding and eternal weight of glory. Death was changed. Instead of a gloomy shadow enveloping the end of all things, it had become the gateway into a world of light. Duty was changed. Instead of an impossible compliance with an inexorable law, it had become a new obedience, with Divine help to accomplish it. They felt that they had received power in the inner life to become the sons of God. And the chief element in this power, according to their own testimony, was the sense of deliverance from the weight, the curse, the condemnation of their sins, through the work of the Lord Jesus Christ.

It is of this strange and wonderful feeling of salvation from sin that I wish to speak more particularly, not as a doctrine, not as a theory, but as an actual fact wrought by Christ in the inner life of man.

1. The normal Christian experience, as it is expressed by those who stand nearest to Christ, utters itself, first of all, as a great sense of peace with God through something which Christ has done to sweep away the barrier of sin between the human and the Divine.

Nowhere else in the world do we find such a deep and keen sense of sin, and of its "three deadly facts," as Henry Drummond calls them, — its power, its stain, and its guilt; nowhere else in the world do we find these facts so clearly recognized, so profoundly felt, as in the New Testament.

In many of our modern religious writers this sense of sin seems to be a vanishing quantity. Mr. Gladstone says: "They appear to have a very low estimate both of the quantity and the quality of sin; of its amount, spread like a deluge over the world, and of the subtlety, intensity, and virulence of its nature." It is chiefly in the secular writers, the dramatists like Ibsen, the novelists like Thomas Hardy, that we find a full and clear recognition of the facts of moral evil to-day. And they offer no remedy, give no hope.

But when we turn back to the New Testament we come into touch with men who faced the facts, and, at the same time, felt that they had found the cure.

Nothing that Jesus said or did led His disciples to minimize or disregard sin, to cover it up with flowers, to transform it into a mere defect or mistake, to deny its reality and explain it away, to say

"The evil is naught, is null, is silence implying sound."

The whole effect of His mission, whatever form it may have taken, whatever its teaching may have been,—its undeniable effect was to intensify and deepen the consciousness of sin as a fatal thing from which men must needs be saved. "If we say we have not sinned," wrote John, "we deceive ourselves and the truth is not in us." "When I would do good," cried Paul, "evil is present with me. O wretched man that I am! Who shall deliver me from the body of this death?"

But with this overwhelming sense of sin which Christ brought into the inner life, He brought also an equally great and deep sense of deliverance from it. "If any man sin," continues John, "we have an advocate with the Father, Jesus Christ the righteous; and He is the propitiation for our sins, and not for ours only, but also for the sins of the whole world." And Paul answers his own bitter cry for deliverance with the words, "I thank God through Jesus Christ our Lord."

2. Now it is an extraordinary thing that men should speak thus, in one breath condemning themselves and in the next breath declaring their freedom from condemnation. And when we come to look into this strange utterance of the inner life, we find that it flows from a twofold experience.

First, there is a profound, unalterable conviction that the life and death of Jesus Christ are an expression of the forgiving love of God towards man. The old idea of God as a stern, angry, revengeful being, demanding the death of the sinner, and delighting in it, has vanished from the inner life of the true Christian. Somehow Christ has blotted it out. Somehow the Christian knows that God is love. And if we ask how he knows it, the answer is that the Only-begotten Son came forth from the bosom of the Father to reveal Him. "Herein is love, not that we loved God, but that He loved us, and sent His Son to be the propitiation for our sins." "God commendeth His love towards us in that while we were yet sinners Christ died for us." All the meaning of Christ's life and death, with us and for us, hangs upon His being the true Son of God, the word of God, the brightness of the Father's glory and the express image of His person. It is this that makes us sure that God is not a fierce, vindictive, relentless God. He is more than a ruler, a judge of all the earth, an almighty king: He is our friend, the lover of our souls. He is willing to live among us, to suffer with us, to die for us.

The entire significance of Christ as a revelation of Divine Love depends upon His real oneness with the Father, and the essential voluntariness of His sacrifice. It is not a punishment inflicted from without, by the inexorable law of God. It is a revelation made from within, by the immeasurable love of God, showing mercy at the heart of righteousness.

This is what makes it an atonement; this is its reconciling power. It is not done to produce a change in the mind of God, but to reveal what was always in His mind, to show how He really feels towards sinful men.

It does not reconcile God to the world. No need of that. God has loved the world forever.

It does reconcile the world to God. Great need of that. For it breaks down the barrier of fear and mistrust; it rends the veil of dreadful dreams that sin has woven before the Divine face, and discloses the countenance of a pitying, forgiving Father; it moves men to repentance by the mightiest force of mercy; it binds men to holy living by the enduring bonds of gratitude and love.

3. But could the sacrifice of Christ mean this much to the inner life of man unless it

also meant something more? Suppose for a moment that we could discover that it was not really a necessary sacrifice; that there was no reason why He should suffer, except perhaps that His sufferings might move our hearts; that His death was nothing more than the accidental consequence of His being entangled in a world like this; that God could have forgiven sin and would have forgiven sin just as well if there had been no crucifixion on Calvary. What then? Would Christ still have the same atoning power to draw our hearts to God?

It is love that reconciles. And it is self-sacrifice that reveals love. But does an unnecessary sacrifice, a useless sacrifice, reveal love in a way that moves and compels our hearts? No. The man who holds his hand in the fire, merely to prove his devotion, may say that he does it for your sake, but he does it really for his own sake. But the man who gives up his life, to rescue you from an actual peril, commands your love because he is your saviour. The crown of love is service. The glory of sacrifice is usefulness. The love of Christ, the sacrifice of Christ, draw their deepest power upon the inner life of man from the conviction that they really have accomplished the deliverance of sinners from the guilt and curse and doom of sin.

This is the testimony of the New Testament. This is the second element in that joyous experience which filled the inner life of the disciples with confidence in Jesus as their Saviour. I do not attempt to explain it, nor did they. But here is the fact. They felt that Jesus put away sin by the sacrifice of Himself. They felt that His offering of Himself upon the cross in our human nature actually wrought a change in the relation of mankind to the divine law and the eternal righteousness. It was a sin-offering, an atoning sacrifice. It was a redemption, a ransom from slavery. It was a satisfaction, the payment of a debt. "He bare our sins in His own body on the tree." "He redeemed us from the curse of the law, being made a curse for us."

This, beyond a doubt, was the interpretation which the Christians put upon the death of their holy Lord and Master on the cross. This was the effect that it actually wrought in their inner life. They did not deem it an accident or a catastrophe. It was not the defeat, nor merely the termination, of His work. It was the crown and consummation of His work. It gave Christ to them more than it took Him from them. They did not think that He died in vain. His death for sinners was the greatest service that love could perform. It accomplished and declared God's righteousness in the remission of sins that are past. It made it possible for God to be just and the justifier of him which believeth in Jesus.

Now, what were the secret laws and what were the mysterious relations of the world to God which made the offering of the sinless life of Jesus necessary for the rescue of mankind from sin, no man knoweth, nor can any man explain them and set them in order. But their existence does not depend upon our knowledge of them. Nor is the satisfaction of them rendered unreal by our ignorance of the way in which they are satisfied. If God is indeed as lofty a being as the moral ruler of a universe must be, it is not to be expected that we should be able to fathom the necessities which are present to His mind. There must be a world of eternal laws and wants and needs lying about us of which we can form no clear conception. Into this world Christ entered by His death. Whatever was needed there for the forgiveness and blotting out of man's sin He provided. Whatever the law required for its righteous vindication He performed. It was the Father's will that He should die to redeem men; and so He died, and men were redeemed.

4. How, then, does this redeeming sacrifice present itself in the inner life of man? One thing is sure. In this region there is no room for anything that is merely formal and artificial. There is no room for what Phillips Brooks calls "the fantastic conception of the imputation to Christ of a sinfulness which was not His, of God's counting Him guilty of wickedness which He had never done."

There is no legal fiction in the real atonement.

God is not a maker of fiction, nor can the inner life of man be satisfied with formalities.

The human heart revolts at the idea of the punishment of the innocent in the place of the guilty. Those instincts which lie deeper than all reasoning are insulted and wounded by the thought of an unwilling and unoffending victim dragged to the altar to suffer for the offenses of others. All that is sincere in human nature recoils from the dogma that pardon and favor and forensic righteousness are to be received on such terms.

And, indeed, there is no trace of such thoughts, such ideas, such dogmas, in the religion of Jesus. They belong to paganism, to fetichism, to the cruel, sensual religions of Mexico and Africa. Shadows of their darkness have fallen upon the outer form of Christianity. Strange and uncouth words have found their way into the dogmatic books which vainly seek to reduce life to logic. Wild and wandering phrases of bewildered theologians have represented Christ as exposed to the Divine wrath in our place, or as "wiping away the red anger-spot from the brow of God." Dismal echoes from the chants of blood-stained heathen temples have crept into the hymns of the church, — echoes which say that

> "On Christ Almighty vengeance fell
> Which must have sunk a world to hell,"

or that

> "One rosy drop from Jesus' heart
> Was worlds of seas to quench God's ire."

These echoes, these phrases, these words, have

undoubtedly penetrated, in a wavering and uncertain way, into the ritual, the dogma, the outer circle, of Christianity. It seems as if, to use the expression of that great German theologian, Rothe, " in His work for man it were the constant fate of God to be misunderstood." But these misunderstandings have not entered into the inner life where Christ is truly manifested as the living sacrifice and saviour. In all the utterances of those men who first felt His redeeming sway there is no trace of them. They received the atonement, they rested upon it, they felt no moral objections to it, because as it came to them it brought no moral objections.

There was no infliction of punishment upon the innocent instead of the guilty. There was no transference of the merits of the sinless to the sinful. Christ remained guiltless; man remained guilty. But Christ entered into humanity, freely, willingly, taking on himself all its limitations, burdens, pains, and services. Christ lived and died with man and for man. He was not a substitute, He was a representative. He was not thrust into our place, He shared our lot; and if that sharing involved a sacrificial death upon the cross, if there was no other way in which He could be one with sinners, and make them one with Himself, and lift them out of guilt and doom, save by dying for their sins, what then?

Does the recognition of this, as a mysterious fact revealed in the crucifixion, cast any stain upon the justice of God? Not so thought Christ, who shrank from the cross, yet said, "Father, not my will, but thine be done." Not so thought the apostles, who saw in Christ crucified the perfect revelation of the righteousness and love of God. Not so thought such a Christian as Phillips Brooks. The inner life of Christendom finds a true expression in his sermon on "The Conqueror from Edom."

"My friends," he says, "far be it from me to read all the deep mystery that is in this picture. Only this I know is the burden and soul of it all, — this truth, — that sin is a horrible, strong, positive thing, and that not even Divinity grapples with him and subdues him except in strife and pain. What pain may mean to the Infinite and Divine, what difficulty may mean to Omnipotence, I cannot tell. Only I know that all that they could mean, they mean here. This symbol of the blood bears this great truth, which has been the power of salvation to millions of hearts, and which must make this conqueror the Saviour of your hearts, too, the truth that only in self-sacrifice and suffering could even God conquer sin. Sin is never so dreadful as when we see the Saviour with that blood upon his garments. And the Saviour himself is never so dear, never wins so utter and so tender a love, as when we see what it has cost Him to save us. Out of that love born of His suffering comes the new impulse after a holy life; and so, when we stand at last purified by the power of grateful obedience, binding our holiness and escape from our sin close to our Lord's struggle with sin for us, it shall be said of us that we have 'washed our robes and made them white in the blood of the Lamb.'"

5. This is the testimony of all who have entered most deeply into the joy and peace and power of the religion of Jesus in the inner life. The suffering and sacrifice of the cross are necessary to save men. The offering of Christ is a mystery made to meet a threefold mystery, — the existence of sin in

God's world, the condemnation of sin by God's law, and the guilt of sin in God's sight. And it is by Christ's willing offering of this real sacrifice that He becomes the Prince of Peace in the inner life.

I turn back to Christ's own words and hear Him saying, "The Son of man came to give his life a ransom for many." "The bread that I will give is my flesh, which I will give for the life of the world." "Except a corn of wheat fall into the ground and die it abideth alone, but if it die it bringeth forth much fruit." "I, if I be lifted up, will draw all men unto me." "This cup is the New Covenant in my blood which is shed for many for the remission of sins."

I turn back to the apostles, and I hear them saying, "Christ died for our sins and was delivered for our offenses. He put away sin by the sacrifice of Himself. By one offering He hath perfected forever them that are sanctified. He hath redeemed us from the curse of the law by being made a curse for us. His blood cleanseth us from all sin. Unto Him that hath loved us and washed us from our sins in His own blood, and hath made us kings and priests unto God and His

Father, to Him be glory and dominion forever and ever."

I turn back to the history of the church and I find the cross of Christ, the emblem of the world's shame and reproach, become the symbol of Christian faith, the treasure of Christian hope, the banner of Christian victory. How came it to be thus transformed? What strange miracle has exalted the instrument of death to the place of glory?

When Christianity came to China under this banner the Chinese wondered at it, mocked at it, issued an edict against it. This edict said: "Why should the worshipers of Jesus reverence the instrument of His punishment, and consider it so to represent Him as not to venture to tread upon it? Would it be common sense, if the father or ancestor of a house had been killed by a shot from a gun, or by a wound from a sword, that his sons or grandsons should reverence the gun or the sword as their father or ancestor?" It is a searching question; and the only answer to it is in the inner life where the cross of Jesus has been planted as the tree of peace and blessing, the sign of divine forgiveness and human love; so that the first cry of faith is

"Simply to Thy cross I cling,"

and the last breath of prayer is

"Hold Thou Thy cross before my closing eyes."

6. I turn to the literature of Christianity, and I find there the same experience of peace with God, through the atonement of Christ crucified, uttered in a thousand ways, expressed in a thousand forms which rise spontaneously out of the varying characters and conditions of men. For this is the strange thing, the beautiful thing, the vital thing, about this experience. It is not possible to reduce it to one fixed and final statement. It is forever changing, and growing, and expanding, because it is a living experience, an ethical reality, an element of the moral life. And as a man's thought of sin and his knowledge of sin are deepened by living, as his idea of God and his fellowship with God are purified and uplifted by believing, so his sense of reconciliation with God through Christ must grow purer and deeper and loftier to keep its place in his inner life.

You come to a man with your theory of the atonement, and he says, "Yes, perhaps it means that to you, but it means something else, something far more precious, to me."

You come to another man, and he says, " No doubt there is truth in your view, but it is not all the truth. Christ crucified means more than that to me." And so it ought to be, so it must be, if the real place of the atonement is in the inner life. We ought not to expect, we ought not to wish, that it can ever be defined or explained in a formula valid for all men and for all time. Whatever it may be in itself, whatever it may be in its objective relations to God's government of the world, for us it must be a progressive, growing, expanding element of spiritual consciousness.

But the reality of it, the pacifying, illuminating power of it, does not change. It runs like a thread of light through the literature of Christianity.

If I had to name the three books outside of the New Testament which lie closest to the Christian heart, and are entitled to be called the classics of Christian faith, I should choose "The Imitation of Christ," and "The Pilgrim's Progress," and "The Christian Year." There is no difference between them in their testimony to the power of the cross of Jesus to save men from sin.

"Take up, therefore, thy cross," says Thomas à Kempis, "and follow Jesus, and thou shalt go into life everlasting. He went before bearing His cross, and died for thee on the cross, that thou mightest also bear thy cross and die on the cross with Him."

"So I saw in my dream," says John Bunyan, "that just as Christian came up with the Cross, his burden loosed from off his shoulders and fell from off his back, and began to tumble, and so continued to do, till it came to the mouth of the sepulchre, where it fell in, and I saw it no more. Then was Christian glad and lightsome, and said with a merry heart, He hath given me rest by His sorrow, and life by His death."

"Is it not strange," says John Keble in his poem on the Crucifixion, —

> "Is it not strange, the darkest hour
> That ever dawned on sinful earth,
> Should touch the heart with softer power
> For comfort than an angel's mirth?
> That to the cross the mourner's eye should turn,
> Sooner than where the stars of Christmas burn?
> . . . . . . . . .
>
> "Lord of my heart, by Thy last cry,
> Let not Thy blood on earth be spent:
> Lo, at Thy feet I fainting lie,
> Mine eyes upon Thy wounds are bent;
> Upon Thy streaming wounds my weary eyes
> Wait, like the parched earth on April skies.

"Wash me, and dry these bitter tears;
Oh, let my heart no farther roam, —
'T is Thine by vows and hopes and fears,
Long since. Oh, call Thy wanderer home, —
To that dear home, safe in Thy wounded side,
Where only broken hearts their sin and shame may hide."

7. This, then, is the testimony of the ages in regard to the message of Christ to the inner life of man. He came to bring the sense of peace and pardon, deliverance from the power and guilt and stain of sin, a true reconciliation with the just and holy God and a new vision of His rescuing love, through the mystery of His sacrifice for us, by His agony and Bloody Sweat, by His Cross and Passion, by His precious Death and Burial. And this is what the atonement has actually done. It has set the conscience free from guilt. It has lifted the burden from the soul. It has made men feel that there was still a chance for them. It has broken the bonds of the rigid and pedantic notion of justice which crushes the heart to the earth, and brought into the inner life the presence of a God who is great enough and good enough to take away sin by bearing it Himself. It has diffused through the soul the fragrance of a new kind of forgiveness, —

the only real forgiveness, — a forgiveness which not only blots out guilt, but restores fellowship, — a forgiveness which says to the forgiven: "Christ was crucified with thee, that thou mightest be crucified with Him. He died for thee, that thou shouldest not henceforth live unto thyself, but unto Him who died for thee and rose again. Rise with Him into the new life. Never despair. Never surrender to remorse or fear or death. Come up with Christ, come on with Christ, into the ransomed life."

Is such a gospel as this a low gospel, a narrow gospel, an immoral gospel, an obsolete gospel, a gospel to be ashamed of in the presence of learning and refinement and moral earnestness? Let men whose hearts have been cleansed and ennobled by it — the men like Paul, and Augustine, and Francis of Assisi, and Martin Luther, and John Wesley — make answer.

Is such an experience as this an unreal experience, a fantastic thing, a thing of no great consequence, of no large influence in

> "The very world which is the world
> Of all of us, — the place where in the end
> We find our happiness, or not at all"?

Let the triumph in the midst of sorrow, the courage in the face of death, and the steadfast devotion to every noble cause, of those who have learned to say, " The life that I now live in the flesh I live by the faith of the Son of God, who loved me and gave Himself for me," make answer.

Is such a mission as this to the inner life of man no longer needed, no longer of value in these latter days of enlightenment, in these high places of culture? Let the unchanged, struggling, sinful heart of man make answer.

Burdened with the weight of responsibilities to which we have never lived up, disenchanted by the sad advance of a knowledge with which our vital wisdom has not kept pace, stained and dishonored by sins of selfishness and pride and impurity and unbrotherliness and greed and avarice and anger, which our very privileges charge with a tenfold guilt, — delicate and self-complacent offenders, men who know but do not, heirs of all the ages who have bartered our birthright and declined our duty and sinned against light a thousand times, — how stand we in the sight of God, my brother-men, without a Saviour from our sins?

Is this an easy age, a careless age, a peaceful, secure, sin-free age for the inner life? On every side, with growing knowledge, the shades of the prison-house close around us. The moralists tell us of ever-increasing obligations, — duties, demands of personal and social righteousness. The standard rises, but the inspiration sinks. Students of life tell us of the permanence and power of evil, the taint of blood, the corruption of nature, the force of degeneration, the heavy fetters of heredity. We need a God with us to set us free. Philosophers tell us that there may be a God, but that He is certainly distant, impersonal, unknown, unknowable.

Ah, what an age for a Divine Redeemer, a liberating God incarnate, a real atonement to deliver us from the coil of sin!

> "Far and wide, though all unknowing,
> Pants for Thee each human breast;
> Human tears for Thee are flowing,
> Human hearts in Thee would rest."

Is there not a welcome in the world to-day for the Conqueror from Edom? Is there not a mission still in our inner life for the Son of God, who loved us and gave Himself for us?

> "The very God! think, Abib; dost thou think?
> So the All-great were the All-loving, too, —

So through the thunder comes a human voice
Saying, 'O heart I made, a heart beats here !
Face, my hands fashioned, see it in myself !
Thou hast no power, nor mayest conceive of mine,
But love I gave thee with myself to love,
And thou must love me who have died for thee !'"

# VI

## THE MESSAGE OF CHRIST TO THE FAMILY

BY THE RT. REV. HENRY C. POTTER, D.D.

# THE MESSAGE OF CHRIST TO THE FAMILY

"God setteth the solitary in families." — PSALM LXVIII. 6.

"Then Jesus . . . came to Bethany, where Lazarus was : . . . there they made him a supper, and Martha served." — ST. JOHN XII. 1, 2.

OF the first of these two verses the story of human society is the enduring verification. "Is it too much to say," asks a gifted student of science, who added to his scientific attainments the higher gift of a seer,[1] — "is it too much to say that the one motive of organic Nature was to make mothers? It is at least certain that this was the chief thing she did." "Run the eye for a moment up the scale of animal life. At the bottom are the first animals, the Protozoa. . . . The Cœlenterata follow; then, in mixed array, the Echinoderms, Worms, and Mollusks. Above these come the Pisces, then the Amphibia, then the Reptilia, then the Oves, then — what? The

[1] Drummond, *The Ascent of Man*, pp. 266, 267.

Mammalia, the Mothers. There the series stops. Nature has never made anything since." " Ask the zoölogist what, judging from science alone, Nature aspired to from the first; he could but answer, Mammalia, — Mothers."

Have we ever thought, now, what must follow from this? In the upward struggle of life from its primitive form, there is at first enormous profusion, — enormous waste, as we should say, — and, at any rate, a purely individual struggle for existence. But as fast as the various forms of life climb higher and higher, as organisms become more complete, as wants become more various, as being becomes more interrelated, there come, finally, the conditions out of which emerge dependence on the one hand, and maternal care and tenderness on the other. We climb the ladder a step higher, and, as reason and intelligence are added to the other endowments of living things, we find a race, a tribe, an order of beings, — call it what you please, — which has developed instinct into forethought, wants and appetites into forecast, the nest or the cave into a house, the need of warmth and shelter into food stored away, and a fire kindled, and clothing pieced, however rudely, together; and all the various needs and anticipations and activities which these involve. As these grow out of the earlier chaotic life, the need of prescience, order, something like what we call thrift — the life and prowess and leadership of the hunter abroad and the ruler at home — appear, and you have developed the father, — the father with authority, added to the mother with tenderness and watchfulness and unselfishness; and the children, as the object of all these; and so at length you have the family.

There are those who believe that there is no God behind all this, and with such I may not argue. But with those of us who are unable to believe otherwise than that all the unfolding of life, in so much of the universe as we know, implies a divine and creating Mind behind it all, the whole becomes coherent and clear.

And this conviction is only deepened and strengthened by what we know of families, of nations, of races. One of these there is whose story is told us in a literature which has survived all revolutions and outlived hundreds of centuries, in which the place of the family in a divine economy is at once central and supreme. You may regard the Hebrew sacred writings as you please; you cannot deal with them at all without finding yourself straightway confronted with the family as an ever-present and potential factor in their history, their poetry, their social and civil enactments. All authority starts there, at once for its definition and its illustration. Back and forth flies the shuttle that weaves the web of that wonderful old Israelitish life; but, interwoven with it all, is the order and the imagery of the family. The home is the centre from which emerge Abram, and Jacob, and Joseph, and Samuel, and David; and each conspicuous and distinctive figure that gives to all those wonderful pages their unique charm and their perennial interest, — Isaac and his sons, Hannah and hers, the lads and maids, the homes so primitive and the loves so passionate, — what is the spell, so strong and so imperishable, which speaks to us through all these, but that of an institution which is divine, and which, in the mind of God, is bound up forever with the progress and well-being of the race?

It is not surprising therefore that, when the most Unique Being who has ever crossed the threshold of an earthly existence takes up His abode among men, He should recognize an institution so august and heavenly in its origin, and consecrate it forever by His own most intimate relation with it. "Born of the Virgin Mary!" The Creed of Christendom rings the solemn mystery round the world on every Christmas morning, and thenceforward whensoever we recite the common symbol of its faith; and as we gather round the Manger Cradle in the Bethlehem stable, mankind kneels down beside the lowly Judean Mother, and before her God-descending Son! Find me, if you can, in all the range of human history, in all the treasures of its letters or its art, in all the legends of its earlier or its later days, a story so resistless in its pathos and its power! We take up its slender thread from the moment of the Annunciation and follow it onward, and with what exquisite beauty, with what inexhaustible significance, it unfolds! We stand looking at Holman Hunt's great picture of the Carpenter Shop with its shadow of the Cross, and not even that shadow moves us more deeply than that sublime self-emptying with which Omnipotence effaced itself and the Son of God became the Son of Mary and of Joseph. Out of that young subjection we behold how mightiest strength and surest wisdom and divinest love grew up into the flower of their perfect youth and manhood; and, remembering the narrowness, the poverty, the intellectual limitations, the undiscerning companionships, of that Nazarene life, we get a new vision of what the discipline of the home may be and do for man.

The wonderful Being who for nearly thirty years dwelt in that home never, indeed, created one for Himself. The reason for this is plain enough in view of the relation which He had come to sustain to all homes and all families, and, through these, to all mankind. But you cannot take up the story of Christ's life among men without being at once impressed with the way in which, a homeless man Himself, He recognized, honored, and loved the home and the family. In that at Nazareth He spent thirty out of the thirty-three years of His earthly life. In another home He wrought His first miracle; into others He followed the sick and the bereaved; and in others still, disesteemed if not despised of men, as in that of Zacchæus and in that other in which, to an age dominated as have been other ages by the social exclusiveness of the so-called "respectable" classes, He gave the scandal to them, the enduring lesson to us, of eating and drinking with publicans and sinners. And then, as if to crown the large and beautiful significance of all the rest, there comes the home in Bethany, with its enduring types of character in all ages, Lazarus, sick unto death; the mystic Mary; and she who, somehow, I think, most interests most of us to-day, Martha, solicitous, care-hindered, and not without a note of querulousness in her eager, anxious voice, but with voice and act shot through and through with the golden thread of self-forgetting love. No student of the life of Jesus has ever quite put into words — the task is too delicate and subtle for words — the relations of the close of that life here to that Israelitish village home; but no reader of the Gospels can fail, I think, to perceive how the Divine Master turned to it more and more frequently, as the great crisis of His life and work drew on, to gather strength for that crisis, and, touching there those human hands and drawing near to human hearts, thus to prepare Himself for that supreme loneliness out of which at last He cried, "My God, my God, why hast Thou forsaken me?"

To such an estimate of the family as all this implies, I am not insensible that the times in which we are living are, in many aspects of them, most unfriendly. The civic and social order of our day, and especially of our land; the theories of life which have among us a wide and increasingly aggressive propaganda; the recoil from restraints and conventions which, whatever of good our fathers found in them, we have come, many of us, to regard as largely or wholly evil; the gradual but steadily increasing weakening of the marriage tie, with its increasing and really appalling disparagement in some quarters of the Divine sanctions of that tie, — all these influences have combined to make the family more and more an institution to be indifferently regarded in itself, and distinctly disparaged as to its obligations and its authority.

There is one explanation for the whole tendency, and it ought not to be difficult to recognize it. " All our modern notions and speculations," said Dr. Horace Bushnell in that remarkable book of his, " Christian Nature," " have taken on a bent toward individualism. In the state, we have been engaged to bring out the civil rights of the individual; asserting his proper liberties as a person, and vindicating his conscience, as a subject of God, from the constraints of force. In matters of religion, we have burst the bonds of church authority, and erected the individual mind into a tribune of judgment within itself; we have asserted free-will as the ground of all proper responsibility, and framed our theories of religion so as to justify the incommunicable nature of persons as distinct units. But, while thus engaged, we have well-nigh lost, as was to be expected, the idea of organic powers and relations. The State, the Church, the Family, have ceased to be regarded as such according to their proper idea, and become a mere collection of units. A national life, a church life, a family life, is no longer conceived or perhaps conceivable by many. Instead of being wrought in together, and penetrated, to some extent, by historic laws and forces common to all the members, we only seem to lie as seeds piled together, without any terms of connection save the accident of proximity, or the fact that we all belong to the heap. And thus the three great forces which God has appointed for the race are, in fact, lost out of mental recognition. The conception is so far gone that, when the fact of such an organic relation is asserted, our enlightened public will stare at the strange conceit, and wonder what can be meant by a paradox so absurd." [1]

Well, what has come of it? For the time has come when, if I am to say any really timely or helpful word, it must be a concrete and not an abstract word. And so I would answer that, among the other freaks and eccentricities of our modern social order that have come of it, we have the modern young girl. She has early left her home, plain, homely, and obscure as are, after all, most human homes. She has found it dull and irksome; she has found its tasks narrow and elementary. She has found its life, she tells you, mean and colorless. She has read a mass of that cheap and tawdry literature

[1] Bushnell's *Christian Nature*, pp. 91, 92.

which is preëminently the product of our own generation and country; and every silly ambition and every grotesque imagination that could find a lodgment in any weak and undisciplined mind has made a home in hers. Perhaps there was not much wisdom, or tenderness, or discernment in that earliest handling of her which she had in the home into which she was born; but, no matter, God put her there. He who ordaineth that "the solitary shall be set" — expressive word — "in families" has created that oldest institution of His inspiration for her ordering and guidance. And— Well, she has resented its restraints, and despised its conditions, and as early as she dared, has flung out of its fellowship. You miss her after a while, — you who had some chance knowledge of her, and whose lines of life, it may have been, crossed hers in some slight and transient way from time to time, and you ask where she has gone. Alas, the truthful answer would have to be, sometimes at any rate, whether our dainty modern agnosticism believes in such a place or no, that she has gone to hell! Certainly she has gone to physical and mental and moral ruin; and out of the far distance comes the echo of her note of wandering despair, "I have no home!"

Nor only such an one. Out of this exaggeration of individualism, which is a feature of our age, we have also the modern young man, with his early impatience of the restraints of home, and with his early endeavor to break out of them. We have him when he is in the gristle, "without understanding, without natural affection, proud, a boaster, an inventor of evil things, disobedient to parents:"[1] tragic coincidence that, when the apostle paints that awful picture of the vices that had rotted the Roman Empire to its core, this is the trait with which that characterization culminates! And we have, too, our modern young man, too often, when he has hardened into the bone of early manhood, — impatient of the life of the family or of its burdens, applauding himself that he is clever enough to evade both the relations and the responsibilities of a home by some corrupt arrangement which will leave him, when he has reached middle life and determines in some thrifty interest to marry, with every finer instinct blunted and coarsened, — sor-

[1] Romans i. 30, 31.

did, cynical, soured, and suspicious: a man without faith; with no single high enthusiasm; the scorner of all things that are "pure and honest, and lovely, and of good report."

From such an one we turn to those fathers of the republic who made our nation great, and to the simple and heroic homes in which their children were reared. Read the story of the boyhood life of Ezekiel Webster, of his sisters and their father and mother, and of the greater brother, Daniel. See in such a story, which was in substance the story of home life throughout your own earlier New England, what reverence for authority there was, what high ideals, what uncomplaining sacrifice, what fidelity to duty, and, shining through them all, what mutual love and tenderness. If there were patriots, and scholars, and saints, and soldiers of high and bright renown, what wonder that it should have been so, with such a nurture to make them!

And so I come to you to-night, my brothers, to commend to you the preciousness and sanctity of the family. One cannot look into the faces of this congregation without thinking of the tremendous potentialities that are bound up, in this particular connection, in the futures of our American young men. In a little while you will be stepping forth into the larger arena of life, and will find yourselves confronted with all the grave and imminent issues that touch the heart of our modern social order. You will have to make up your minds and take your stand with reference to questions which as yet, it may be, you have scarcely thought of, — the constitution of the family; the value and obligation of its various ties; and the relation of those ties to the permanence, purity, and saneness of our social order. One of the most urgent of these questions is that which relates to the character and the sanctity of the marriage tie. I may not discuss it here; but as I am speaking of *the Message of Christ to the Family,* I must ask you to recognize with what singular and exceptional explicitness Jesus delivers Himself concerning this matter. As a rule, you know, His method, if I may call it so, was otherwise. He laid down great principles, but He declined, ordinarily, to concern Himself with their application.

Here, however, His course is quite different. "In the matter of divorce," as Professor Shaler Mathews in his admirable volume on "The Social Teaching of Jesus"[1] has said, — "in the matter of divorce Jesus has left us some of the most explicit legislation that the Gospels have preserved. . . . The ground for this definiteness is not difficult to discover. Marriage, both in its lower and its higher aspects, is the basis of family union. Family life is the most sacred of all relations outside the relation between God and man. . . . To disclaim this first of human relations is to loosen the bonds of society; to lower present social ideals; to do injury to the essential nature both of the man and the woman. . . . We are not now concerned with the practicability of such an ideal. It may be too absolute for our imperfect society. But it can at least be suggested that there are grounds for hesitation before one admits that the spirit animating this part of the social teaching of Jesus has been materially surpassed by much of to-day's divorce legislation."

I commend such considerations to your serious thought. Whatever may be the dominant note of the airy persiflage of the hour concerning home and the family, and our

[1] *The Social Teaching of Jesus*, pp. 86–91.

various relations to them, no questions touch more closely or deeply the fundamental interests of human society. In a little while many of you to whom I speak this evening will be dealing, in your homes, your professions, your personal or legislative responsibilities, with what, in many ways and through many influences, affects the family and the home. Remember, then, that there is no school like it in all the world for educating high ideals, and developing a lofty type of character. Dr. Bushnell, in the volume to which I have already referred, points out, in the history of our American forefathers, how early the marriage relation was entered into. There was not, in those cases, the selfish thriftiness on the one hand, or the self-indulgent improvidence on the other, which in our own times are doing so much to discourage the foundation of a family. And, most of all, — will it seem unchivalric to say it in an assemblage in which they are so largely absent? — neither was there, on the part of women of culture and of a more or less delicate nurture, so marked a disposition to leave the burdens of the family maintenance to be so largely borne by one of the partners of the marriage compact. If it is, and was, the duty of the husband to support his wife, it was recognized in a singularly fine and heroic and uncomplaining way that it was, no less, in her measure and according to her ability the duty of the wife to support her husband, — by her sympathy, by her courage, by her cheerful sharing of every burden that could be shared, by her wise frugality, by her brave acquiescence in straitened conditions, — in one word, by her wifely devotion and by her motherly self-effacement, thrilling and illuminating every tie and every task! And out of this mutuality of love and service there came to us that fine race of mothers whose sons and daughters were the joy and glory of our earlier history.

We know what made them so brave, and strong, and tender. They drew great inspirations for the founding and building of their families from the divinest of all sources. Not for nothing was it, most surely, they discerned that the one supreme, dominant, and enduring figure of the Kingdom of God among men was the image of a Family. God was a King, indeed, but He was most of all a Father. Christ was a Saviour and a

Redeemer, verily, but He was to be no less our Elder Brother. The Church was His Kingdom, supreme and preëminent among all the kingdoms of the world, but it was equally and always His peerless and precious Bride. And the law which ruled within that Kingdom was to be forever the law of filial love and loyalty.

Fair and incomparable image! Patriarch and apostle, singers and prophets of the elder and the later time, and, high above them all, the divinest Voice of all, take up that one clear note, and lift us by means of it to the vision of the life that is to be. "In my Father's house," says Jesus, when the time has come for Him and His to part out of the earlier and inferior relation of companions, — "in my Father's house are many mansions. I go to prepare a place for you, — you, whom I call no longer servants but brethren, — that where I am there ye may be also!" There, whatever else of earthly and human institutions vanishes out of the realm and the life that are to be, the family in its highest and most absolutely perfect type will still endure.

Cherish it then, my brothers, in that earlier

but no less divine form of it in which you and I have our various shares to-day. Honor its authority, reverence its sanctity, prize and cultivate its intercourse. For so, when ties so dear and precious here are sundered, out of its discipline, out of its fellowship of mutual love and trust, out of its joys and sorrows, each so sacred and unique, may we hope to pass into the house and the home " not made with hands," — into the presence of " the God and Father of us all," thence to go no more out forever!

# APPENDIX

# APPENDIX

*Extract from the Secretary's Report of the Class of 1885 of Harvard College.*

## WILLIAM BELDEN NOBLE.

BORN in Essex, N. Y., October 17, 1860. Died at Glenwood, Colo., July 27, 1896.

The sudden death of our classmate, while visiting the mountains of Colorado in search of health and rest, has brought a deep sense of sadness to those of the Class of 1885 who knew and loved him. His earnestness of purpose, purity of character, and faith in God and man so impressed itself on all his friends and associates that this small tribute to his memory is offered to the class as in some measure expressing their feeling of loss through his death.

William Belden Noble was the only son of Belden Noble and Adeline M. (Ferris) Noble, and from early youth lived with his family in Washington, D. C.

His first collegiate work was done at Princeton, where he passed one year before entering Harvard in the Class of 1884. He entered at once into the life of the College, in the full vigor of youth, and with the highest ideals of his duty to the world and his fellow men. He applied himself conscientiously to his studies, and at the same time, as long as his health permitted, spent considerable energy in athletics and literary work.

He played on his Freshman Class football eleven, and on the University lacrosse twelve, of which he was also the captain for a time.

His literary tastes made him an earnest and constant writer for the "Crimson Bi-Weekly," the daily "Herald Crimson," and for outside papers, while his social life found expression through his membership of the O. K., the Institute of 1770, the Δ. K. E., and the Hasty Pudding Club.

But his close attention to his studies, together with his other interests in the life of the University, proved too great a strain, and in his Junior year he was obliged to leave the University on account of nervous prostration.

After resting for a year, he returned to Cambridge in the Senior year of our class, and, although not in good health, took up his studies again, and was graduated among those of the highest rank of the Class of 1885, receiving honorable mention in English, English Composition, and Political Economy, and being entitled to a dissertation as a Commencement part.

The dissertation which he delivered was upon Faith, a fitting subject for one whose whole life and thought were consecrated to Truth and guided by Faith.

After graduation he passed some time in travel and in the care of his father's estate. In 1887 he was married to Miss Nannie Yulee, of Florida, who, with their only child, Yulee, survives him. In 1888 he returned to Cambridge with his wife to prepare himself for the ministry, and studied for two years in the Episcopal Theological School. His health, however, would not permit him to continue his studies, or to do active work, and for the last few years he had traveled constantly with his family in a hopeless search for health.

Everywhere, those who met him were impressed with his fine personality, and inspired by his spiritual, guileless life. Only the day before his death, just as he was leaving his ranch life in Colorado to join his family in the East, he wrote to his devoted wife : " I live in the ever-present consciousness of my God, so near, so loving, and so great."

That expression was the undertone of his life, the spiritual growth of that faith which he hoped to teach. In all his intellectual pursuits, his wife gave him full sympathy, and together they strove after the same ideals. His constant thoughts were a fervent prayer and thanksgiving, " reaching out his eager and quickened faculties to the spiritual world around him."

W. H. B., Jr.

The Riverside Press
CAMBRIDGE, MASSACHUSETTS, U. S. A.
ELECTROTYPED AND PRINTED BY
H. O. HOUGHTON AND CO.

www.ingramcontent.com/pod-product-compliance
Lightning Source LLC
Chambersburg PA
CBHW031818230426
43669CB00009B/1180